Social Work Skills with Adults

Social Work Skills with Adults

Edited by ANDY MANTELL

Series Editors: Jonathan Parker and Greta Bradley

First published in 2009 by Learning Matters Ltd

British Library Cataloguing in Publication Data

A CIP record for this book is available from the British Library

ISBN 978 1 84445 218 7

Cover design by Code 5 Design Associates Ltd
Project management by Deer Park Productions
Typeset by PDQ Typesetting Ltd
Printed and bound in Great Britain by Bell & Bain Ltd, Glasgow

Learning Matters Ltd
33 Southernhay East
Exeter EX1 1NX
Tel: 01392 215560
info@learningmatters.co.uk
www.learningmatters.co.uk

Mixed Sources
Product group from well-managed
forests and other controlled sources
www.fsc.org Cert no. TT-COC-002769
© 1996 Forest Stewardship Council

FSC

Contents

Part 3 Professional accountability and competence

Editor and contributors

The following are all members of the Social Care and Social Work Team, Faculty of Sports, Education and Social Sciences, University of Chichester, with the exception of Teri Cranmer, Rebecca Long and Graham Tooth.

Gill Constable is a Senior Lecturer in Social Work.

Teri Cranmer is Social Care Professional Lead (mental health) for West Sussex Social Services.

David Gaylard is a Senior Lecturer in Social Work.

Colin Goble is a Senior Lecturer in Social and Health Care.

Barbara Hall is the Project Coordinator for 'Skills for Care' in Sussex.

Rebecca Long is a trainer in the voluntary sector.

Andy Mantell is a Senior Lecturer in Social Work.

Janet McCray is Principal Lecturer in Social and Health Care Leadership.

Marie Price is a Senior Lecturer in Social Work.

Terry Scragg is a Visiting Fellow.

Chris Smethurst is Deputy Head of the Social Work Department.

Graham Tooth is Senior Practitioner and Training and Development Officer for West Sussex County Council.

Acknowledgements

I would like to thank the contributors and their families. I would particularly like to thank Fiona Collins for her exceptional support with proof reading and the staff at Learning Matters for their unstinting help, especially Luke Block and Kate Lodge. Finally, I would like to thank the service users, carers and practitioners who have shown us the way.

This book is dedicated to Rachael – I know you prefer flowers!

Introduction

Social work skills define the distinctive nature and determine the effectiveness of social work practice. Many of these skills are generic and can be transferred to a wide range of social work practice settings. Whether you are working with young people or an older person, you are usually working with families and their life cycle. However, social work with adults has its own distinctive challenges that influence the skills that social workers need to develop. Unlike social work with younger people, social work with adults is guided by a complex raft of legislation spanning over half a century. Practice has evolved and continues to follow and to shape policy, which has shifted from paternalistic protection to promoting rights and choices. The personalisation agenda (DoH, 2008a and DoH, 2008b) offers a significant challenge to social workers' skill sets. It requires a change from directing to empowering. This will necessitate the development of new skills but also provide the opportunity to rediscover aspects of social work neglected within the era of care management.

Social work skills are required not just within direct work with carers, people who use services and other professionals but also in constantly managing and updating our own practice. This book is written primarily for the student social worker and explores the range of skills that are essential in social work with adults and that will be useful across the whole of your programme of study. It will in turn enable you to gain an understanding of ways to meet current challenges in the field that will also be invaluable in subsequent years when you move into practice as a qualified social worker, particularly if you are working with adult service users. Likewise, experienced and qualified social workers will also find that the book provides an overview of social work skills with adults and discussion of a range of perspectives that can inform and refresh their practice.

Book structure

This book is written by staff of the Social Work and Social Care Team, University of Chichester, and colleagues from the Independent Living Association and West Sussex Adult Services. As you will see below, the book starts with an exploration of the skills for interacting with adults who use services: engaging, communication and empowering practice. The second section of the book explores the skills necessary for effective social work interventions: assessing, decision-making, collaboration and negotiation. Finally, the last four chapters focus on you, your professional account-ability and competence. They explore how you present yourself in writing and person, how you reflect on your practice and skills for your self-management.

Part 1 – Interacting with adult service users

Chapter 1 examines the essential interpersonal skills involved in the process of enga-ging with others. The chapter particularly focuses upon creating effective one-to-one relationships. It explores establishing rapport, listening, developing trust, being clear about the aims of our interventions, maintaining momentum and managing endings.

Chapter 2 builds from Chapter 1 to explore the communication skills necessary for nurturing effective relationships. It applies the skills that promote open one-to-one communication to challenging areas of practice. Particular attention is paid to situa-tions that may challenge our attitudes, may be distressing or can be threatening. In doing so it illustrates the importance of non-verbal communication, silence and reflec-tive practice.

Chapter 3 explores the attitudes, knowledge and skills necessary to promote empow-erment and participation. It then considers how social workers can act as advocates, identifying the tensions and practice dilemmas and the need to explicitly recognise the social worker's power. This chapter addresses the difficulties social workers can face in promoting anti-oppressive and anti-discriminatory practice, with particular reference to the social model of disability and the experience of people with learning disabilities.

Part 2 – Intervening with adult service users

Chapter 4 examines the assessment process and how it is linked to the broad reper-toire of social work skills. The chapter highlights the contentious nature of assessments and how they can be led by procedures, needs, rights and risks. Risk assessment as a central aspect of adult social work is then considered in more detail.

Chapter 5 explores the building blocks for effective decision-making in social work with adults. It considers the impact of competing evidence and opinions and empha-sises the importance of values and anti-oppressive practice in shaping effective decisions. It aims to equip you with an understanding of the skills necessary for appraising and applying evidence in complex decision-making situations and provides pointers to caring for yourself in this often stressful process.

Chapter 6 identifies the components of good collaborative practice, including: valu-ing roles, knowledge of different contexts, building trust, delivering and being credible, managing boundaries, and conflict management. Collaboration as a prac-tice action is explored while other language and terms often used interchangeably are clarified. Key policy and legislation, general protocols and practice requirements are critically reviewed and barriers to collaboration are considered. During the chapter attention is paid to ethical frameworks to aid anti-oppressive and appropriate social work practice.

Chapter 7 reviews the negotiation skills necessary for effective social work practice. Negotiation is an integral but often overlooked aspect of social work. This chapter will provide an exploration of the skills that can be utilised to facilitate and influence negotiations. In so doing it highlights the risks, conflicts, ambiguity and ethical dilemmas that can accompany negotiations.

Part 3 – Professional accountability and competence

Chapter 8 considers the report-writing and recording skills required of social workers in adult services. This neglected area of social work practice has been the subject of numerous reports from public inquiries that have highlighted the need for better case recording. This chapter identifies what makes for effective case recording, what should be included and what to avoid. This exploration situates written communication in the context of the societal, organisational and professional significance attached to documents and ethical and value considerations such as confidentiality and the power of documents.

Chapter 9 focuses on how workers present themselves. However, it moves beyond simply considering your physical appearance to explore the impact of your behaviours, thoughts, belief systems and values on your practice. Self-presentation is considered as part of your developmental journey where your destination is to become a competent, empathic and reflective practitioner.

Chapter 10 explores how to develop reflective practice, the essential component of competent and safe practitioners. It provides an overview of its main elements and what it means in social work practice with adults. It considers some of the potential benefits from using this technique and offers you practical ways that you can develop your reflective thinking.

Chapter 11 considers the skills required for self-management. The pressures of current social work practice require students/practitioners to be efficient and effective at managing their time, often needing to respond to competing priorities. This chapter considers some of the skills relevant to your 'survival toolkit' in the changing social work environment. At the heart of the chapter are the concept and implications of the 'psychological contract' between the employer and the employee, and the role of the GSCC Code of Practice for Employers and Employees. The chapter also looks at practical approaches to reduce stress, issues concerning time management, and an exploration of the management of change.

Learning features

This book is interactive, drawing on practice-based examples and research to aid your learning. You are encouraged to work through the book as an active participant, taking responsibility for your learning, in order to increase your knowledge, understanding and ability to apply this learning to your practice. You will be expected to reflect creatively on how your immediate learning needs can be met in working with adult service users and how your professional learning can be developed in your future career.

We have devised activities that require you to reflect on experiences, situations and events and help you to review and summarise the learning undertaken. In this way your knowledge will become deeply embedded as part of your development. When you come to practise learning in an agency, the work and reflection undertaken here will help you to improve and hone your skills and knowledge.

This book intends to develop your skills in social work with adults, but we realise that there many other sources of information that you may wish to access that provide more detail on specific aspects of work with adults and we have suggested further reading at the end of each chapter for you to follow up.

PART 1
INTERACTING WITH ADULT SERVICE USERS

Chapter 1

Skills for engagement
Andy Mantell

A C H I E V I N G   A   S O C I A L   W O R K   D E G R E E

This chapter will help you to meet the following National Occupational Standards:

Key Role 1: Prepare for, and work with individuals, families, carers, groups and communities to assess their needs and circumstances.

- Work with individuals, families, carers, groups and communities to enable them to analyse, identify, clarify and express their strengths, expectations and limitations.
- Work with individuals, families, carers, groups and communities to enable them to assess and make informed decisions about their needs, circumstances, risks, preferred options and resources.

Key Role 2: Plan, carry out, review and evaluate social work practice, with individuals, families, carers, groups, communities and other professionals.

- Develop and maintain relationships with individuals, families, carers, groups, communities and others.
- Reduce contact and withdraw from relationships appropriately.

This chapter will also help you achieve the following key social work benchmarks (Quality Assurance Agency for Higher Education, 2008):

- An ability to use this knowledge and understanding to engage in effective relationships with service users and carers.
- Demonstrate habits of critical reflection on their performance and take responsibility for modifying action in light of this.

Introduction

Social work involves working with people. At the heart of that enterprise is the quality of the relationships that we establish. This chapter will explore how we develop relationships with people; how we engage with them. The nature of these relationships and their significance to practice then provides the context for exploring skills in engaging with people. After clarifying the meaning and media for engaging, the process for developing good relationships will be explored in more detail. Communication (see Chapter 2) can be seen as critical for developing and sustaining relationships and is at the core of the subsequent chapters. Engagement, however, provides the social lubricant for effective communication.

Building relationships

We live in a social work climate increasingly concerned with outcomes and the evidence base to produce those outcomes. In such an atmosphere it is easy for the humble relationship to be overlooked. Yet it does not matter if you have the most effective tools to hand, if you do not build good relationships with your clients, your colleagues and other agencies, the experience and outcome of your interactions are likely to be less successful.

RESEARCH SUMMARY

Lessons from counselling
Boisvert and Faust (2003) in an interesting analysis of studies into the effectiveness of counselling found that people change more due to common factors than to specific factors associated with therapies and that 10 per cent of people will actually get worse as a result of therapy. Crucially, the relationship between the therapist and the client is the best predictor of treatment outcome and is more important than the approach selected (Boisvert and Faust, 2003, p511).

Comment

Considering these findings in relation to social work raises some interesting points. You are unlikely to ever find a method of practice that will always work. Instead you will need to be eclectic, assembling a toolbox of well practised methods that you can apply in different situations (Trevithick, 2005).

Most significantly, your relationship with the person, rather than the method you adopt, will be the better determinant of the outcome of your intervention. Emphasising the therapeutic importance of relationships marks a revisiting of social work's psychodynamic roots. However, as Lefevre (2008) points out, contemporary practitioners should consider the person in a wider social context, incorporating an understanding of anti-oppressive practice and empowerment.

While interventions have great potential to help carers and people who use services, the stigma attached to contact with social services departments together with overly procedural approaches have great potential for harm. Social workers focused entirely on gathering facts, rather than how and when we explore people's often traumatic experiences, are likely to be viewed by carers and people who use services as intrusive and uncaring. Failing to engage with people will inhibit the exchange of information and undermine our assessments and subsequent decision making (see Chapters 4 and 5).

ACTIVITY *1.1*

Admirable qualities
Write down the five most important attributes or qualities you appreciate in others.

Comment

The points that you identified may have included openness, respect, honesty, reliability and being non-judgmental. Unsurprisingly, carers and people who use services also value these qualities and those attributes such as warmth and humour that display the human aspect of the professional (Lefevre, 2008, p90). However, while we appreciate these behaviours we can have a high degree of tolerance depending on our expectations of a particular relationship. You may, for example, consider reliability as an absolute in a partner, but not in a casual acquaintance. In our interventions with carers and people who use services, we understand how they may have limited experience of receiving or giving these attributes that nurture positive relationships. However, our tolerance of the lack of such qualities will depend on factors such as the nature and stage of our intervention and the needs of the individual. For example, in working with Paul, a 24-year-old man who misused substances, his respect had to be earned over time and his level of honesty and reliability gradually followed.

Changing roles, changing relationships?

In the same way that we require different methods to suit different situations we also need to employ a range of relationship styles to suit the situation and the role we are undertaking. Howe (1994, p518) summarised social workers' roles in terms of care, control and cure. However, there has been a continued shift towards a less paternalistic state, with people managing their own care (Department of Health, 2006, 2007, 2008a). This has been accompanied by an increasing tension between a culture of rights and risk aversion (see Chapters 3 and 4). Since then the language and corresponding emphasis in practice have shifted in adult social work so that 'care' has translated to the more detached 'care management', 'control' has become 'protection' through risk assessment and management (see Chapter 4) and 'cure' has transformed into 'change' through empowerment. Braye and Preston-Shoot (1995) have argued that to achieve empowering practice, social worker relationships should be based on consultation, i.e. clients influencing the decision-making process; participation, i.e. clients' active involvement; partnership, i.e. power and responsibility sharing; and control, i.e. respecting the autonomy of the individual.

CASE STUDY

The nature of empowerment?
Sharon Day is a 42-year-old Afro-Caribbean woman who suffers from bipolar affective disorder (manic depression). She is married to Raymond (47), who also suffers from mania, and they have a six-year-old daughter Faye. Ms Day became suicidal following a long period of depression. Mr Day struggled to support her and look after Faye. Ms Day was compulsorily admitted to a psychiatric unit under the Mental Health Act 2007 and given ECT against her will.

Comment

You may be surprised to hear that Ms Day was pleased that she was detained and that she received ECT. At that point she felt out of control and unable to manage and was grateful to services for 'taking over'. However, following the course of ECT she wanted to regain control and return to her family with minimal support.

If Ms Day had received proactive support she may never have required such extreme reactive intervention. Her situation consequently also demonstrates how targeting services at those in greatest need can be disempowering.

This is an extreme situation, but it is important to recognise that at different points in our relationships with carers and people who use services we may need to be more or less directive. Often in short-term interventions this follows a progressive pattern but this is not always the case.

While empowerment is a key social work value, operational exigencies such as managing limited resources can encourage directive crisis interventions. Policy has shifted from a directive to a more empowering role for social work (DEMOS, 2008). Unfortunately, *a gap exists between the rhetoric of government policy and the reality of practice* (Cree and Myers, 2008, p134). The prevailing ethos of managerialism means that practitioners have actually been spending less time in face-to-face work with carers and people who use services (Leveridge, 2002). If practitioners do not have the time to engage with people, it is difficult to see how they can be attentive to their concerns and develop empowering practice (see Chapter 3). It will be interesting to see, as the lexicon of adult social work discussed above continues to shift towards 'care navigation', 'safeguarding' and 'empowerment' respectively, if social workers will become more engaged with face to face practice once more.

Working alliances

While it is necessary to employ a range of relationship styles in social work, a preferred model remains the working alliance (Greenson, 1967). The relationship is based solely on the role that we are performing for its existence, but it can be more than a *relationship-as-means-to-achieving-desired-outcomes* (Egan, 2007, p49). It can provide a space where a person feels safe, valued and able to reflect on their situation. Rogers (1951), in his client-centred approach, developed the notion of the therapeutic relationship in which the person can be supported to reach their full potential. He considered such relationships to require unconditional positive regard, i.e. valuing the person regardless of their actions; congruence, i.e. genuineness; and empathy (see below). Client-centred practice is an example of a non-directive approach in which the *relationship-in-itself* (Egan, 2007, p49) has intrinsic value.

While social work has been more directive than Rogers' therapeutic approach, an effective working alliance can combine the values of therapeutic relationships (see research summary below) and the benefits of the relationship as a vehicle for achieving goals. As Hudson and Sheldon (2000, p65) observed: *A good working relationship is a necessary but not sufficient condition for being an effective helper.*

RESEARCH SUMMARY

The values of effective relationships

Egan (2007, p56) in his well-respected guide to helping people, expanded Rogers' core values to identify five key elements in helping relationships.

- **Respect** *This includes respecting and taking seriously the views of carers' or people who use services, and in social work often advocating for those views to be heard. This does not mean collusion and may necessitate challenging them. In working with people we should not manipulate, exploit or coerce carers or people who use services. Respect for those we work with also places a responsibility upon us to continue to develop as a competent practitioner. Being competent and committed, Egan (2007, p56) noted, is not simply the point you have reached at graduation (or indeed after your post-qualifying training): it is an ongoing process.*

- **Empathy** *Sensing and responding to a person's inner world (Rogers, 1975).*

- **Genuineness** *The congruent practitioner should be present in the moment, open, spontaneous and not defensive. They should listen and communicate without distortion (Egan, 2007, p56). They should be striving towards a relationship that is not based on dependence or counter dependence (Egan, 2007, p56, after Gibb, 1968 and 1978).*

- **Empowerment** *Enabling clients to identify, develop and harness their resources to change their lives (Egan, 2007, p57, after Strong, Yoder and Corcoran, 1995).*

- **A bias for action** *Egan argues that successful intervention should aim to produce an outcome in which the clients become doers rather than mere reactors, preventers rather than fixers, initiators rather than followers (Egan, 2007, p61).*

Comment

While you may view these values as more relevant to therapy than social work, they nevertheless have considerable merit. If we take Egan's (2007, p61) *bias for action*, the quote included could be a sound bite for the new agenda for change within health and social care.

One of the significant differences between Egan's (2007) model and social work is that in a social work intervention there may be several clients: the person who uses services, their carer, their children and the state. Often social workers have to balance competing needs and interests when determining whose take priority. Greater genuineness, transparency and accountability would be achieved by explicitly distinguishing who is actually the primary client, at a given time.

Social work also goes further than enabling people to gain the confidence and competence to be able to take control of their lives and marshal their resources and social capital to change their circumstances. Social workers also aim to make people aware of their rights to advocate on their behalf and directly challenge the institutions, such as housing, which affect their lives.

What do we mean by engagement?

You will have a relationship, good or bad, with everyone you work with, but some relationships will be much better; you will feel more connected. You will have rapport. Rapport is *the state of harmony, compatibility and empathy that permits mutual understanding and a working relationship between the client and the social worker* (Barker, 2003, p359). Engaging is about developing rapport. Engaging continues throughout a relationship, but is most essential in the early stages, as the old adage points out: *You never get a second chance to make a first impression.*

Some elements of rapport are thought to be unconscious. Transference, for example, is where a person's way of relating to someone in their past is replayed with another person. As Lefevre (2008, p84) notes: *it may feel at times as if there is a real dissonance between who you are intending to be and who the client experiences you as.* As practitioners we also bring our own counter-transference to relationships with carers and people who use services. This may be an emotional and psychological response to their behaviour or it may be derived from our own relationship history. Transference and counter-transference are not necessarily negative emotions but unwarranted positive responses can also become damaging when expectations cannot be fulfilled (Lefevre, 2008).

Your ability to establish rapport can also be inhibited by your mandate, for example, compulsorily detaining someone under the Mental Health Act 2007 may produce superficial co-operation or no engagement. Rapport may also suffer due to you making a mistake. In extreme situations failing to engage may result in the carer, person who uses services or worker requesting a change in practitioner.

Each intervention adds to your learning and ways of managing difficult situations. Mistakes can happen, but the competent practitioner reflects and learns so that they do not recur (see Chapter 10).

ACTIVITY *1.2*

Ways of engaging
List the different means of communicating by which you engage with people, for example, face to face conversation.

Comment

Any means of communicating with other people benefits from the degree with which we engage with the recipient. This includes via communication aids, using an intermediary, by phone or in writing. This chapter will focus on one-to-one involvement, because the skills are generally transferable to other situations. However, a few points are worth noting.

Engaging people by telephone removes the non-verbal cues to your attitude and feelings (Lishman, 1994) that can facilitate engagement, making you more reliant on your speed of speech, tone of voice and use of language. Writing by email or letter denies tone and consequently requires even more careful consideration of language. A sentence that is softened by your intonation can appear harsh on the page. When writing letters or reports, think about the purpose of your communication and ensure you adopt the appropriate level of formality. Always remember that these texts still need to engage the reader to hold their attention (see Chapter 8).

When working with someone who uses a communication aid, for example an alphabet board or a light writer, try to ensure that you have gained some familiarity with this form of communication prior to meeting the person; it may be necessary to have someone accompany you who is familiar with the system. Interacting via a communication system can easily become a barrier between you or it could be a shared activity in which you are engaged towards a common purpose. It is easy for such experiences to be disempowering for the service user and for the carer. It can, for example, be tempting to finish what a person is trying to communicate, but this can deny their voice (see Chapter 2). The same applies to people whose speech is impaired.

If you have to communicate via an interpreter, this creates an immediate barrier to your engaging with the carer or service user. For example, working with a deaf man with mental health problems, I found that my body language was ignored as he focused on the professional interpreter, who was completely neutral and failed entirely to engage him. Keeping your speech brief will increase the interaction between the three of you and reduce the possibility of mistranslation. Wherever possible, avoid involving family members or members of the community to interpret as this can inhibit open communication or alter the conversation towards their agenda.

Preparation for developing one-to-one relationships

Successful engagement with anyone can be facilitated by planning and preparation. The more you know about a person, the better placed you are to plan for the most likely eventualities and prepare for meeting them. Reading the file notes can provide invaluable background information, such as the person's social history and previous experiences of social work intervention. It is consequently essential that these records are clear, concise, coherent and above all accurate (see Chapter 8). Working on a hospital ward I would always check with the charge nurse before seeing a patient, even if I had been working with the patient for months. As well as a courtesy and promoting multi-disciplinary working (see Chapter 6), this ensured that I had the most up-to-date information.

> ### CASE STUDY
>
> *Credible assessments*
> *Rita Brown was a 44-year-old woman with Huntington's disease (a rare, degenerative, neurological condition) whose case records stated that she was aggressive and non-co-operative. She lived in a one-bedroom flat, the floor of which was covered in magazines to a depth of about 8 inches. On meeting her, she lurched up to me so that she stood very close and spoke in a slurred voice while waving her arms at me.*

Comment

From the information I had received it was prudent to visit her accompanied by a colleague and on entering her flat I was careful to ensure that my path to the exit was clear. However, it is important to caution against over-reliance on what you are told and have read before you meet someone. Her slurred speech, arm movements and inability to judge appropriate proximity were all due to symptoms of her Huntington's disease. However, I did need to be aware that her arm movements were involuntary and that she might hit me accidentally. She obsessively bought cookery magazines and as she found her mobility was becoming unsteady she had put them on the floor to provide cushioning in case she fell. Her 'unco-operativeness' was due to her not wanting a care worker to remove them and her tendency to go out if the care worker was late. I explained to the care agency that people with Huntington's disease can develop rigid thinking, which in her case meant that if a person said they will visit at 8 a.m. they had better be there then, not ten or twenty minutes later.

This case study demonstrates how lack of understanding and respect of a person's situation and failings in services, i.e. poor punctuality, can wrongly be ascribed to people who use services. This is not to say that information should be ignored or not sought, but that we should approach people with an open mind rather than an empty one (Strauss and Corbin, 1994). The more perspectives that we can gather the better our understanding is likely to become.

Introductions

The circumstances, place and manner of our introduction to a person are likely to affect the rapport that we develop. High-stress situations for the carer and the person who uses services can accentuate how you are responded to. This may be a positive or negative effect depending on whether you are identified as an ally or a threat.

The environment in which you meet can also have a major influence upon the quality of your subsequent relationship. Meeting in the person's home can feel safe and empowering for them, whereas a police cell is likely to feel intimidating. However, statutory involvement, such as mental health assessments, can be experienced as an invasion of the privacy and sanctuary that home symbolises. A person with mental health problems once told me that while they needed interventions at times, they wished they could all occur away from their home.

Environments obviously need to be accessible to disabled people and to people for whom English is not their first language. I once worked for a social services department which had leaflets for complaining about the service in 12 different languages, but leaflets about how to access the service were only in English.

ACTIVITY 1.3

Welcome?

Think about the lobby and waiting room where you are working. How welcome would you feel if you were a carer or person who uses services coming to the office for the first time?

Comment

If the meeting is at a social services office, then how welcome are people made by the attitude of the staff? If the decor is dingy and neglected, how safe or comfortable will they feel? For example, I once visited a social work office and was waiting in the scruffy waiting room with one other person. On the table was one out-of-date gossip magazine that added to the general effect of neglect. A woman came in and after a brief conversation with the receptionist through the security glass, started shouting and swearing. The receptionist retreated, leaving anyone in the reception area to fend for themselves.

The manner in which we are greeted discloses a significant amount about the expected nature of the relationship, from the person whose first words to me were *F*** off!* to the offer of tea and cake. As Lishman observed: *They frequently arrive at a social work agency with a sense of stigma or shame and suspicious, hostile or fearful expectation* (Lishman, 1994, p6).

Remember that rituals of greeting vary from culture to culture, so try to ensure that you are informed about the cultural and religious practices of the person you are meeting. Simple acts like shaking hands can create or remove boundaries. Similarly, the inappropriate use of either someone's first or surname can be a considerable cause of offence, particularly if you get their name or the pronunciation wrong. Older people may be offended by the informality of first names or younger people uncomfortable with the formality of surnames, but as a general rule ask rather than assume. It is, however, essential to confirm who they are, who you are and why you are meeting them.

Use of self

When you meet with someone they are not just meeting a professional, they are also meeting you. Feeling that they are meeting with a real person and not a professional persona is crucial to carers and people who use services engaging with social workers (Clarkson, 1990). Lefevre (2008) argues that detached objectivity is a fallacy: we cannot help but bring ourselves to the relationship. However, use of self needs to be carefully monitored to ensure that the purpose of the relationship is not shifted to meeting our needs rather than theirs.

Who we are has a significant impact on how people will respond to us. It is important that we understand not just how we view ourselves but also how others view us. We must remain aware of how factors such as our profession, gender, sexuality, age, ethnicity, religion, class and accent can instantly endear us to or alienate us from another person. Sometimes it can be important to acknowledge such factors; however, sometimes we have to recognise the vagaries of interactions. For example, on my first visit to a 19-year-old man with learning difficulties, he ran to me and threw his arms around me. His mother had stood frozen to the spot and then relaxed and said: *Oh that's good! He bit the last social worker.* I never did find out why he decided to hug rather than bite me.

We can have more control over other factors, such as our dress, but our cultural backgrounds may still determine the level of freedom that we experience in our dress codes. What you wear may have a strong link to your sense of identity. However, it is important to weigh your individuality against the role you are performing and the context. If you are representing a person in court, it is important that you engage with the court as a credible professional. If you present yourself in a casual manner your evidence may be undermined (see Chapter 9). Choices of clothing can also significantly reduce your risk of injury in difficult situations; for example, ties and dangly jewellery can easily be grabbed accidentally or on purpose.

In considering ourselves we need to explore how we feel about the emotive events in life which are often the precursor to our involvement in people's lives. For example, cancer, dementia, AIDS and death remain taboo subjects for some people. Those we work with may be trying to make sense of their situation, while facing ignorance or stigma and discrimination from those around them. We need to explore and become aware of our own feelings and thoughts prior to being confronted by them when we meet those we are supposed to help. We must also be careful to go at their pace, not our own, when exploring such issues and at times recognise that such discussions may be 'off limits'.

Your knowledge base plays a significant role in your understanding of situations and the confidence that people then develop in you. Carers and people who use services often feel isolated, but knowing that you have an understanding of some of the challenges that they face when, for example, a family member has an acquired brain injury, can help to reduce the sense of being alone, facing the unknown. However, it is essential that we acknowledge when we do not know, but make it clear that we will find out, rather than making assumptions.

Body language or non-verbal communication (NVC) is important as it may convey our thoughts, feelings or mood to others. While this may not always be conscious, with practice and self-awareness you can identify and avoid habitual patterns, such as drumming fingers, which can imply boredom (see Chapter 9). Ideally your body language will be open and receptive, relaxed but attentive, not casual. Awareness of NVC can sometimes help you to identify the mood of a carer or service user far more effectively than their verbal communication. If you are working with someone who has difficulty or is unable to communicate verbally, reading their NVC is essential. Sensitivity to NVC can also help you to realise when you are mirroring the body language of others. Used expertly and judiciously, mirroring can become a deliberate act to create a sense of connection between you; it can also be used to modify behaviour. For example, if you are both tense and you start to relax, they may mirror that behaviour. It is also important to note that body language is culture specific and consequently highly susceptible to misinterpretation. They may, for example, view your body language as not being interested or not taking them seriously or interpret your mirrored tension as an aggressive response.

It is important to remain sensitive to their body language but also to the instinctive responses of your own body and autonomic nervous system. If a carer or service user is aggressive towards you, your body will react. Your fight-or-flight impulse will be triggered and your body will release adrenaline, your pulse will increase and your breathing is likely to become more shallow. It is therefore very important to consciously relax and breathe more deeply – this will help reduce your anxiety and fear. At the same time this projects the message that you are not scared or being aggressive, both of which can trigger violence (see Chapter 9). Such NVC is picked up and responded to far more readily than your verbal communication in conflict situations.

Hearing their story

The purpose of our intervention will influence the relationship that we are likely to develop. However, in engaging with people we need to have an openness which goes beyond that purpose, as the intervention may change as our assessment goes beyond the presenting problem. The quality of our relationship will dictate how much information a person will disclose. Open, active listening to their concerns will ensure that you gain the most from the information that is shared.

RESEARCH SUMMARY

McKay, et al. (1995, p16) identified 12 inhibitors to active listening.

- **Comparing** *Comparing yourself to the other person. This distracts from actually listening to what they are saying.*
- **Mind reading** *Second-guessing what the person means.*
- **Rehearsing** *Attending to what you will say next rather than to what they are saying.*
- **Filtering** *Focusing on those points that concern you. This can occur particularly if you are too task- or agenda-orientated, leaving you blinkered to hints of other potentially more important issues, or even closing down such discussions.*
- **Judging** *Where a person's views are disregarded due to our view of the person, for example, as being unqualified to comment.*

RESEARCH SUMMARY continued

- **Dreaming** *Where we are attending to our daydreams rather than to what the person is saying.*

- **Identifying** *Where we relate a person's experience to our own and interject our experience rather than listening to theirs.*

- **Advising** *Rather than listening to their whole account it is very easy to cut to offering solutions.*

- **Sparring** *Being quick to disagree rather than listening, or it can take the form of discounting, i.e. refusing to hear what someone has to say.*

- **Being right** *Unable to hear criticism or contrary views.*

- **Derailing** *Changing the topic and in doing so dismissing their view.*

- **Placating** *Being so concerned with comforting or mollifying the person that we fail to listen to them.*

Comment

The tendency to offer solutions before all the issues have been explored is a problem which I have noticed seems to occur particularly within groups. I would also argue that daydreaming tends to occur after we have already become distracted. Your comfort can also be a considerable source of distraction. This may seem too trivial to consider but if you are tired, hungry or need the toilet, all of these factors will distract you from attending to what is being said. Seating and whether you are too hot or too cold can all play their part in blocking your attention. It should be noted that all of these points equally apply to people listening to us.

Active listening is not simply passively hearing but requires that we are focused on the here and now and what is being said. It is not just a vital part of engaging with people but an essential aspect of anti-oppressive practice; to be heard and to be valued. This is a tiring activity but practice enables us to concentrate for longer.

When meeting carers or people who use services for the first time, it is important to give them time to tell their story. Working on a hospital ward with people who had suffered traumatic, life-changing and life-threatening events, I was struck by how few of these people had been given an opportunity to really talk about what had happened to them. Professionals can become preoccupied with their expert intervention, rather than with the individual's experience. Hearing their story can be validating to them and in turn they build their trust in you as a professional. It is at this point that we are starting to build empathy with the person, developing an insight into their world. It is important to draw a distinction between sympathy, i.e. feeling for another person, and empathy, i.e. feeling with another person (Shulman, 1999). This can be a distressing and upsetting experience when, for example, a person talks of how they are losing their loved one to Alzheimer's disease. However, it is important to maintain perspective and purpose. Their loss is not your loss; you are merely a witness to their distress. Social workers are like participant-observers in anthropological fieldwork. If you hold yourself too distant from their experiences, you are likely to be perceived as uninterested, cold or uncaring, but if you become too immersed, then you may lose your professional and emotional boundaries risking emotional burn-out.

ACTIVITY **1.4**

Displaying emotions
Are there any circumstances in which it would be okay to cry in front of a carer or person who uses services?
Does it make a difference if the social worker is male or female?

Comment

Some social workers are unequivocal that there are no circumstances in which this would be appropriate. From this perspective crying can be seen as a breach of boundaries, a loss of control and consequently ability to perform their role. However, others would argue that this privileges instrumental care (caring for) over emotional care (caring about). Fox (1999) advocated that professionals should tend towards emotional care, in order to counter power differentials and avoid becoming too detached from their work. A critical element here seems to be the implied loss of control associated with crying. Crying by men, while growing in social acceptability, still holds a particularly strong risk of alienating people. As a general rule I would argue that it is better to contain your emotions, so that you are fully available to help the service user and do not risk closing them down, as they attempt to protect you. However, you may need to debrief after hearing a particularly harrowing account or one that touches on your own experiences (see Chapter 11). In some cases you might require counselling support.

At times you may need to encourage a person to continue their account. Such prompts can be seen to exist on a continuum from the unobtrusive nod or tilting your head to one side, to a simple *yes?* or *go on?*, to repeating what they have said to the much more directive *can you tell me about?* Silence can be particularly powerful; it can make us feel uncomfortable and inclined to fill the space, but it can also encourage a person to expand further (see Chapter 2). In part this will depend on the culture that we come from as silence can hold negative or positive connotations.

Clarification, negotiation and planning

Having gathered information, it is important to clarify that you have understood correctly. This also provides valuable validation of their perspective. Repeating phrases they have used can help to build connections between you, but it is important that you check that you have shared understanding of those terms.

The information they have provided is likely to have illuminated what they see as the issues and what their expectations are of you. It is important to clarify these points and to identify how they would like their situation to be after the intervention. Negotiation may be required to help them to recognise the implications of issues they may have ignored or been unaware of and to gain agreement to act on these points. Negotiation can be particularly difficult where several people are involved with conflicting agendas (see Chapter 7). It is important that you are clear about your role. At times this will require considerable effort to remain neutral and at other times necessitate explicit clarification that you are advocating for a particular person's perspective.

A key issue to address at this point is expectations. Any relationship you have established will be destroyed if you promise a Rolls Royce and deliver a Mini. However, it is important to not destroy hope. A 24-year-old man who suffered an acquired brain injury told me that it was the positive approaches of his social worker and physiotherapist that had motivated him to keep going. However, we need to be clear and realistic and try to ensure that we are both working towards achievable goals.

Maintaining relationships

While engagement primarily occurs in the early stages of a relationship, it can take considerable work to sustain an individual's engagement over time. This can be the case particularly where the crisis that precipitated the intervention has passed and the drive for change has reduced. Here is where the quality of your relationship and of your empathy with the person can provide motivation and encouragement to remain engaged. Empowering approaches, as well as being desirable, have a real practical advantage as they are based around goals that the carer or service user want to achieve (see Chapter 3).

It is in this part of the relationship that the carer or service user can start to assess your performance – have you proved to be reliable? Maluccio's observation from 1979 (Lishman, 1994, p9) that initially warmth and sympathy are necessary, but later competence and knowledge are required, is still relevant today. If you have not delivered on what you have agreed (never promise), then their trust and engagement with you will understandably deteriorate, regardless of whether or not you have a legitimate excuse.

It is also important to monitor the relationship to ensure that dissonance does not develop between you and the carer and/or person who use services. Even when we think we are working towards agreed goals, it is easy for differences to emerge and the level of engagement to dissipate. For example, I once worked with a 22-year-old man who had cerebral palsy, who wished to enter a care home for younger people. We visited several homes and yet each time there was something different wrong with the home: one was too big, one was too small, one too isolated, another 'too busy'. He also seemed reluctant and slightly resentful of visiting. Speaking with him, it became clear that visiting the first home had made him realise what living in a care home would be like and he had changed his mind and now wished to live in his own accommodation. He had been waiting for the right time to tell me, as he knew I had gone to considerable effort. Reflection in action, i.e. your thinking at the time, as opposed to reflection on action, i.e. your thinking afterwards (Johnsson and Svensson, 2004, after Schön, 1983), can enable you to salvage a situation which would otherwise deteriorate (see Chapter 10). I had been too focused on the plan to fully appreciate the signals he was giving me.

Disengaging

Endings are often neglected yet without them the benefits of a relationship in itself and as a means to achieving a desired outcome can be eroded. At best the service user and the social worker can be left with a sense of unfinished business and at worst the service user may feel betrayed and abandoned. Their self-esteem, confidence and motivation may plummet and successful work on achieving empowerment and bias for action be eroded. One of the main causes may be social workers being task- rather than process-orientated. This may hide a social worker's own emotional difficulties in managing goodbyes.

Goodbyes provide an opportunity to evaluate your intervention and review what the carer or person who has used services has achieved. Closure in this way can facilitate the service user feeling confident to face the future without social work support, but can also confirm a positive experience of social work, if they do require further help. Closure actually begins at the start of our engagement: when we are agreeing what will be the nature of the relationship, we should be starting to cultivate an expectation of our involvement becoming unnecessary (see Chapter 3).

C H A P T E R   S U M M A R Y

This chapter has aimed to explore the skills necessary to engage with adults. It has argued that engaging is the difference between developing an adequate relationship and a good relationship. The quality of your relationship enhances your ability to develop a more thorough assessment and increases the likelihood of achieving successful outcomes, even when managing difficult issues.

The government's review of care and support services (DoH, 2008) has at its heart the nature of the relationship between the state, the citizen, the family and the community.

The inevitable and welcome introduction of individualised budgets across England provides challenges for old systems of delivering services but may release many workers from procedural practices more concerned with gate-keeping than supporting people. *In the past, the relationships we created were considered a central aspect of social work and essential to good practice* (Trevithick, 2007, p7). In the transformation from case managers to care navigators, advisers, guides and brokers it remains critical that we engage with carers and people who use services, if social workers' services are to be not just necessary but welcome.

Egan, G (2007) *The skilled helper* (8th edition). Belmont, CA: Thomson.
A neglected gem, which should be essential reading.

Trevithick, P (2005) *Social work skills: A practice handbook* (2nd edition). Maidenhead: Open University Press.
A comprehensive and critical exploration of the skills required within social work.

Chapter 2

Communication skills
Marie Price

A C H I E V I N G   A   S O C I A L   W O R K   D E G R E E

This chapter will help you to meet the following National Occupational Standards:

Key Role 1: Prepare for, and work with individuals, families, carers, groups and communities to assess their needs and circumstances.

- Work with individuals, families, carers, groups and communities to enable them to analyse, identify, clarify and express their strengths, expectations and limitations.
- Work with individuals, families, carers, groups and communities to enable them to assess and make informed decisions about their needs, circumstances, risks, preferred options and resources.

This chapter will also help you achieve the following key social work benchmarks (Quality Assurance Agency for Higher Education, 2008):

- An ability to use this knowledge and understanding to engage in effective relationships with service users and carers.
- Demonstrate habits of critical reflection on their performance and take responsibility for modifying action in light of this.

Introduction

Communication is the medium for our everyday interactions and consequently is often unconscious and overlooked. Gesture, word, music, smell, touch and environment, for example, all communicate with us and us with them. As you have seen in Chapter 1, good communication skills are essential for establishing the quality of relationships that promote successful social work outcomes. These relationships are not only with carers and people who use services, but also colleagues and other professionals. This chapter will explore communication in situations which can be challenging for us. This may be due to situations being distressing, intimidating or challenging our own world view. It will also raise our awareness of how we need to be sensitive to how we can unconsciously communicate our views and authority, potentially alienating or disempowering those we seek to enable. This in turn will link with the next chapter, which looks at how workers can develop relationships which empower. During this chapter I will explore identified communication skills including the area of keeping emotionally safe, self-awareness, barriers to open communication, hidden messages, spirituality, emotional engagement and keeping physically safe.

Communication skills

In the first chapter five key elements are identified for effective communication in helping relationships, and 12 inhibitors. Many texts aimed at the caring professions, along with your social work training, provide insights into how to communicate well. Margaret Hough (2006, p57) summarised the generic communication skills for effective relationships required in counselling, which can be adapted to social work as follows.

- **Listening** Active attention to what is being said, rather than passive hearing.

- **Observation of non-verbal behaviour** Monitoring and analysing your own and other people's body language. It is through our heightened sensitivity and analysis of gestures, posture and facial expression that we become consciously aware of these often subtle messages.

- **Reflecting back** Repeating back what the carer or service user has said to you or seems to be feeling. This enables them to know that we have heard what they have said and provides them with the opportunity to question it.

- **Paraphrasing** Rewording what they have said, confirming that you have a shared understanding of their situation.

- **Summarising** Précising what they have said can confirm that we have understood their concerns and can serve to clarify what can be complex and confusing information.

- **Asking appropriate questions** These need to be pertinent and sensitive to the situation. Sometimes this can be about choosing the right time to ask a question and at others it can be selecting the right wording.

- **Managing silence** We need to allow silences so that the person we're working with can gather their thoughts, reflect on what they've said and heard, and prepare a response. This skill isn't always easy to manage (see Activity 2.1).

- **Challenging** Used to help a service user to think about their behaviour and attitudes. Confronting these issues in a way that is helpful to the person involved.

- **Immediacy** Being present and not distracted in the moment of the session and using the information and the feelings that are available to us.

- **Self-disclosure** Sharing your own experiences can illuminate a situation or create a sense that you will understand their experience due to your similar experience. However, this can be misleading as you have not shared the same experience. This can produce assumptions that they will feel what you felt and can manage the situation in the same way you have. We all like to speak about ourselves and self-disclosure can easily become about us rather than them. Consequently this is a method to be used with extreme caution if used at all.

It is important to note that some people we work with will require us to take other factors into account to facilitate good communication. For example, if you are working with someone who has cognitive difficulties, such as an acquired brain injury, then you need to ensure that the environment is quiet and without distractions and ensure that you communicate in short, simple sentences, avoiding abstract meanings. A particular difficulty here is that while we tend to use open questions to facilitate gaining an understanding of the perspective of the service user, this often does not work if they have cognitive difficulties. Instead our questions can seem vague and confusing. In these situations it can be more empowering to give them a few clear options from which to choose.

ACTIVITY **2.1**

List all the feelings you have when a conversation dries up and no one is speaking. Do you feel differently if they are close friends, people you are working with or complete strangers?

Comment

You might have listed words like 'punishing' or 'awkward'. These feelings are often related to how silences felt for us as children, when someone was punishing us by not speaking to us or we felt that at school we needed to come up with an answer and weren't able to. Carers or people who use services may share or have very different responses to silence so we need to be alert and aware of what is happening to and for them as well as ourselves. Balancing our divergent needs can be difficult: our discomfort might make us less likely to want to stay with it or if we are very comfortable with silence we might let it go on too long.

RESEARCH SUMMARY

Research undertaken by Beresford, Adshead and Croft (2007) highlights the qualities in social workers that are appreciated by service users. Although the research for the book focused on palliative care, it recognises that these features are equally applicable to all areas of social work. The following areas are considered to be of paramount importance.

- *Being able to determine their own agenda and work in partnership.*
- *Being listened to with a non-judgmental and respectful attitude.*
- *The social worker giving them time and being accessible and available.*
- *The social worker being reliable and delivering promised action.*
- *The social worker being available for both the service user and those close to them.*
- *The social worker having a good level of expertise and a willingness to learn.*
- *The social worker being available to talk about any issue of importance to the service user. This made people feel that their anxieties could be contained.*

Keeping emotionally safe

As expressed earlier, interaction and communication are at the heart of all social work. However, these interactions can have unexpected and sometimes unwanted emotional consequences for us. We need to understand for ourselves in what circumstances this might happen and how we can recognise those feelings for what they are. Interlinked with this is the ability to know ourselves well, including our value base and belief system, in order to provide the best outcomes for carers and people who use services. As social workers with adults we need to provide a safe environment which enables carers and service users to fully express themselves while acknowledging that this may evoke difficult feelings in us. In these situations there is a need to maintain a balance between being open to listening and communicating while keeping ourselves emotionally safe in an appropriate manner. These areas highlight where supervision really comes into its own. Using that reflective space helps us make sense of what we are feeling and how that may impact on our work. Peer support is also helpful. Sharing with others' situations which they too could have encountered or may encounter in the future.

ACTIVITY 2.2

Think about situations that upset you.
In what ways do you protect yourself?

Comment

You may be aware of what triggers an emotional response in you. During your social work training you will be exposed to a range of situations which provoke this reaction. This isn't a sign of weakness but an acknowledgement that you are also human, with all the frailties that implies. Consequently, it is important to become aware of what gets under your defences and makes you feel vulnerable.

While we may be aware of many of these triggers, others may catch us by surprise. This may be because we didn't know they were there or because someone else's story reawakens a situation that we thought we had dealt with. In such situations it is common to exhibit the flight-or-fight response. This can lead to us withdrawing physically and/or emotionally from a situation or potentially becoming aggressive or intimidating. In these situations we need to be careful not to block someone else's communication while ensuring that we do not become so upset we are not able to function or place undue responsibility on the service user. Our responses, of course, are not always solely triggered by our interactions with service users but can be evoked by colleagues and other professionals.

Self-awareness

Self-awareness – recognising what we feel, when we feel it and how we deal with it – is essential for effective communication. Patrick Casement (2002) advocates developing an 'internal supervisor'. This enables the worker to develop an inner ear that attunes itself to pick up information, both from the person being worked with and from ourselves, monitoring how we are and what our responses are, and enabling us to adjust appropriately to situations. This shouldn't replace real supervision (see Chapter 11) but should be developed as a way of monitoring our internal worlds and responses. This gives us the opportunity to enhance how we are able to process and use the information available to make better relationships and decisions.

Should I or ought I?

We ignore how we feel emotionally and physically at our peril; the results can be detrimental to our practice, self-esteem and mental health. Recently I had a bereavement. It was a situation where before the death I needed to spend some time sorting various practical problems, sometimes at short notice. This resulted in my having to occasionally cancel meetings and commitments. After the death of this relative I didn't feel I could cancel any more appointments, so I proceeded to fulfil my obligations despite feeling that I wasn't fully present emotionally and able to communicate as effectively as I might otherwise have done. On one occasion the person I was working with could sense that something was wrong and neither she nor I were able to work in the way that we would normally work. This resulted in us both wasting time and energy and required us to go back and work through the issues we needed to, plus address the difficulties from the previous time we had met. Whereas if I had rearranged the time and come to the meeting available emotionally it would have avoided some of these problems. Similarly, a colleague, despite feeling a migraine starting, decided that she couldn't cancel a teaching commitment or get a colleague to take the session as she 'ought to get on with it'. The migraine affected her performance, causing her to take time from a subsequent session to unpick this interaction and explain again some of the concepts covered inadequately in the previous session.

Our growing self-awareness can enable us to manage anxieties about how we feel we ought to perform and recognise what we should do when our ability to communicate at the high level necessary within social work has been impaired. It is important to realise that the pressure to act can come from our own expectations, those of others or our presumptions about the expectations of others. It is consequently essential to have an honest and open dialogue with yourself and other people involved in the interactions.

It is also important to understand that when carers and people who use services communicate with us, they feel this same pressure between what they need to say and do and what they feel they ought to say and do. Family members can feel obliged to provide care, guilty if they resent the demands of caring and judged if they can no longer manage (Mantell, 2006). People who use services can feel that they have to be grateful for familial care and to act in a passive way. A social worker can be presented with a situation which superficially seems fine, but which is masking increasing conflict. It is in such situations that identifying dissonance between what is said and non-verbal communication often provides the key.

CASE STUDY

Mark, a newly qualified social worker, had been allocated to Sam, who was unable to speak due to an oral cancer that had required major surgery. Sam had not been involved with any services previously and lived in a caravan with limited facilities to cook or store food. Swallowing had become very difficult for Sam, requiring him to liquidise food. He also had to ensure that the nutritional content was high as he was able to eat very little. No one had told Mark that Sam's ability to communicate had also been significantly impaired. He was also not prepared for the emotional impact of seeing Sam's facial disfigurement and he found it hard not to stare.

Mark confirmed that Sam was prepared to write his answers after listening to Mark's questions. This was a frustrating, slow process for Mark, who was conscious that he had to visit another person that afternoon. He tried to speed up the process, asking the next question as soon as Sam had answered the previous one, but soon realised that Sam was becoming fatigued and that his answers were becoming briefer.

Utilising his internal supervisor, Mark was able to reflect on the task and ask if Sam would like a break. He used this space to call his next client and say he would be late. He also managed to get hold of his feelings of disgust, pity and curiosity, recognising them for what they were and to compartmentalise them, while making a mental note to discuss the way he felt with his supervisor.

Comment

As you can see from this example, myriad thoughts and feelings can go through our minds at any one point. It is not that we don't all have them; it's the way in which we respond to them that is important. If we are not self-aware we might let those feelings register on our faces, making it more difficult for the person we are working with to feel accepted, to trust us and be prepared to work with us.

Barriers to open communication

Why then might we be wary of entering or engaging with these situations? Some of the issues we have looked at already but others may be around denial, a refusal to recognise the circumstances that we find ourselves in and possibly a fear that we may get it wrong or get in too deep. The worker may also be working within too rigid a framework or theoretical base with little room for manoeuvre. There could be barriers between the worker and the service user. The barriers could be due to a gender or cultural issue or something personal such as a fear that they will be weighed down by the problem or that they will feel inadequate in dealing with it. In these circumstances it is better to check out your concerns with the service user. Don't be too afraid of getting it wrong – take a risk, but do it sensitively. By taking risks we are able to offer the person we are working with an opportunity to voice their problem. I know that I have always appreciated the people who have been prepared to go that one step further to find a solution or to listen, even when they have been worried or over-whelmed by the information I might be sharing with them.

Hidden messages

One of the other very necessary messages to convey is the art of being non-judgmen-tal. This could be seen as an anomaly, as social work is often about making judgments. However, the issue is to filter out personal views from more objective facts. Personally I feel that we are all judgmental to some degree. We all have areas that we are quick to form opinions about whether they have been influenced by our upbringing or the media or situations we have been involved with. We need to con-stantly monitor how our personal judgments might influence our thinking and our relationships with carers, people who use services and other professionals. For exam-ple, your own experiences of doctors and their media portrayal may leave you in awe of them; or, you may have had negative experiences of doctors and be highly suspi-cious of the medical model. Both perspectives could lead to incorrect assumptions.

Judgments come in all sorts of guises – we may, for example, make them about someone's appearance, the way they speak or their accent. These sorts of judgments are usually made without us thinking about them, part of how we respond on a day-to-day basis. There are other sorts of judgments when we consider someone's skin colour, their religion, their gender or their age. It is worth stopping for a moment here to think about what other sorts of things about a person we can make judgments about; often these are linked to stereotypes and bear little resemblance to reality. We need to consider all aspects of the individual and how we respond to them as being different to us.

ACTIVITY 2.3

Write down messages you were given from childhood about age, skin colour, sexual orientation, gender, culture, race, physical disability, mental health, learning disability, religion.
Which ones do you still believe and why? Which have you rejected and why?

Comment

Some of these ideas were probably handed down to you from parents, care givers, teachers and peers. You may well find that as you have matured and developed and had your thinking challenged on a social work course, you have changed your ideas. Even if they haven't changed, you will have explored those ideas and will know why you believe what you do.

Spirituality

One area which can form a particular barrier to communication and trigger our personal judgments is spirituality. It is important to make the distinction between religion and spirituality. Religion can be described as *the corporate, organized and outward expression of belief systems and an attempt to describe and express faith, ordinarily in community* (Lunn, 1993, quoted in Sheldon, 1997, p23). Spirituality is the essence of what it means to be human, our ultimate existential concerns, questions about meaning and values and our deepest relationships, whether with others, with God or gods, or with ourselves.

So how do we address spirituality with the service users we are working with? First of all we have to have an understanding of ourselves as spiritual beings.

ACTIVITY **2.4**

How do you understand this question in relation to yourself? Do you have a religious belief? Do you have a feeling that there is something bigger than you? How do you answer questions about why we are here or what it's all about? How would you describe the very essence of yourself to someone else? What is important to you?

Comment

Some people describe their spiritual selves as their soul or consciousness, something that is distinct from their body and survives after their body. It is a natural part of being and can be described as humankind's ultimate nature or purpose. Existentialism is part of these ideas which suggests that individuals create their own meaning as opposed to it being created for them.

CASE STUDY

Mary had been diagnosed with a rapidly progressing form of a neurological disorder and only had a couple of months to live. She had two small children, both under the age of three. In my discussions with her the things that were uppermost in her mind were the practicalities of her situation, i.e. how to cope with mobility, feeding herself, keeping clean and all the everyday tasks that she was becoming less able to do. However, under-pinning all of this was the pressing issue of what would happen to her children when she died. She had no partner but did have a very supportive family who had arranged to look after the children when the time came. As time went on and Mary was no longer able to care for herself, the conversations took a different turn and she became aware that the children would have no conscious memory of her voice or indeed what she stood for. We talked about the possibilities and decided that she would record both her voice and messages for the children to enable them to have a sense of who she was and what they meant to her and her outlook on life. Mary was no longer able to hold anything, had a very weak voice and spent most of her days in bed. On a prearranged day and time I made arrangements for a recording device to be placed on her pillow and agreed to

---

> ### CASE STUDY *continued*
>
> check her every few minutes to ensure that the device was still in place and she was still happy to speak into it. She tired very easily so the monitoring was essential to enable her to achieve her goals.
>
> Following the session Mary was able to feel that she had given her children part of herself that she wouldn't otherwise have been able to. The essence of her had been passed on to her children via a recording that will be a lasting reflection of who she was.

Comment

This was a situation where I had to put my own emotions and feeling to one side. At the time my children weren't very much older than hers and the thought of someone having to do that for me was very difficult. It took a considerable amount of thinking through and planning in order for me to be sure that I was doing what was in her best interests. I also had to be sure that it was something that I could manage and be supported to undertake through good supervision (see Chapter 11).

This was also an example of where we sometimes need to take risks with our service users and go that extra mile in order for them to meet their own goals. It would have been easy to say that it was too difficult for me emotionally or to have not heard what she had said or misinterpreted what she wanted to do. This was an exceptional set of circumstances that required careful handling; however, there are many situations where we need to create an environment where people can tell us what they would like and how they would like to live their lives. This may include things they may want to say and express that may be difficult for us to hear. Again this is where self-awareness is important, enabling us to better understand what we can tolerate and what we find difficult. This isn't a weakness, it is a real strength and promotes our own personal development.

It is important to note that if we offer something to a service user and they reject the idea, it doesn't always mean we got it wrong. It sometimes means that they are not ready to hear it yet .We can store it up and present it later, maybe in a different form. However, sometimes we have got it wrong as we are not experts in their lives, only witnesses to their situation as it is now. We need to be kind to ourselves also and tell ourselves that at least we were prepared to try.

Emotional engagement

Both Pam Trevithick (2005) and Janet Seden's (2005) work accept that as human beings we are always communicating something even if we do not always understand what we are giving or receiving. They cite the ability to build relationships as an essential part of the social work role and in order to achieve this effectively communication skills are paramount. Understanding and practising communication are necessary in order to provide the foundation for good relationships and consequently meeting the needs of those we work with. Coupled with this is the ability to work with people creatively, using methods other than dialogue in order to achieve positive outcomes for service users. Both Trevithick and Seden argue that social work is a highly skilled activity and the skills and interventions that we choose should focus on the individual, whether they be service users, colleagues or other professionals. Emotional engagement is the ability to connect with another person on a level that encourages understanding and a willingness to work with whatever the carer or service user needs. Sometimes this can be the situation they may be facing; sometimes it can be a dilemma of one kind or another. Other subjects that are sometimes difficult to tackle may include raw emotions, for example, in Mary's case above, sadness was one of the emotions that was prominent. As human beings we usually shy away from feelings that are going to hurt us or we feel will damage us in some way. Sometimes we might feel overwhelmed by these feelings. Again we need to recognise what other people's feelings and experiences stir up in us and what we do to keep ourselves safe. Go back to the first activity in this chapter and think again about what upsets you and how you protect yourself.

Anger is another emotion that can be experienced as fearful or uncontrolled. Anger is often expressed when people feel unheard or backed into a corner with little power or control over the situation they are experiencing. While steps need to be taken to ensure our safety, we also need to be aware of what is happening for the service user and what steps we can take to alleviate the tension. It may not be our situation to sort out but we can have some understanding of what is happening and attempt to empathise and give back some control to whoever we are working with.

Keeping physically safe

It is important to distinguish between anger, which can be a healthy expression of pent-up emotion, and aggression, which is where that anger becomes focused on a person or object. Working with a person's anger can be an uncomfortable experience but can be extremely valuable in helping a person to move on emotionally. However, if a person becomes aggressive, either verbally or physically, the most important thing is to keep you both safe. A zero-tolerance approach (DoH, 1999a) is recommended, in which you provide the person with clear, calm feedback that you will not accept that behaviour.

It is important, though, to note that most people follow a cycle of escalation in their aggressive behaviour, breaking down their social inhibitors, for example, starting by swearing, moving to kicking objects, before becoming violent towards you. If you give a person a clear, calm message that you will not tolerate their actions, people will sometimes escalate their behaviour to the next level, before de-escalating. So if you consider they are close to assaulting you, withdraw immediately. For some people, however, there are no or limited inhibitors to violence. This can particularly occur where someone has damage to the frontal lobe of the brain, which controls behaviour. Another example of where people may find it difficult to control their anger is when they feel they have no choices or voice in the decisions being made.

CASE STUDY

Ken Tenant

Mr Tenant was a 22-year-old boxer who suffered an acquired brain injury following a fight outside a pub. He could stand with the help of two people and required a wheelchair for mobility. He had right-sided weakness and was unable to speak. He was receiving rehabilitation on a hospital ward. If he became annoyed or upset he would clench his right fist and then punch anyone within range. He was particularly aggressive when staff gave him a shower in the morning. The staff team worked to introduce a routine and cues, such as music, smells and verbal prompts which would help Mr Tenant to understand what was happening to him, but to no avail. His partner explained that he always had his shower in the evening at home. The ward staff changed his shower time to the evening and his aggression around this issue stopped.

Comment

It is easy for people who have been aggressive to be labelled as an aggressive person. A colleague of mine, having worked for several years on a unit for people with challenging behaviour, felt that one of the most important lessons learnt from that experience was that aggressive behaviour communicates something in its own right. That does not make it acceptable, but understanding what a person is trying to communicate is central to preventing the behaviour occurring. The next step is to work with the person to develop more acceptable ways of communicating and getting their needs met.

Often people become isolated and this can increase their sense of vulnerability or hostility. It takes time and patience to work with people in this situation and build their trust. Usually this requires developing clear boundaries with the person, but also showing them positive regard and helping to build their self-esteem.

C H A P T E R   S U M M A R Y

In this chapter we have gone some way to considering what we need to do to meet the needs of the service users we work with and to communicate in a way that is effective and as free from our own clutter as possible. While this is vital in the work we do, we also need to be aware of what is required to keep ourselves safe, both emotionally and physically, and again this chapter has considered how we might evaluate these areas. However, we need to recognise that our fear of new or potentially difficult situations must not stop us from trying to meet the needs of the service users with whom we work. They serve as a reminder that we must be aware of our internal supervisor. We should be able and prepared to take risks and provide opportunities for the people we work with in order to help them lead more fulfilling lives and give ourselves the satisfaction of having done a good job.

FURTHER READING

Beresford, P, Adshead, L and Croft, S (2007) *Palliative care, social work and service users*. London: Jessica Kingsley.
This book seeks to ascertain the views of service users about what they want and need in order for social workers to meet their needs.

Lishman, J (1994) *Communications in social work*. Basingstoke: Macmillan.
This book introduces and examines all forms of communication in a variety of social work settings.

Seden, J (2005) *Counselling skills in social work practice* (2nd edition). Maidenhead: Open University Press.
This book shows how counselling skills underpin social work practice.

Trevithick, P (2005) *Social work skills: A practice handbook* (2nd edition). Maidenhead: Open University Press.
This text provides a toolbox of skills from which to draw and enables us to begin to establish good relationships.

Chapter 3

Skills for empowerment, participation and advocacy
Colin Goble

ACHIEVING A SOCIAL WORK DEGREE

This chapter will help you to meet the following National Occupational Standards:

Key Role 3: Advocacy

Be able to:

- lobby on behalf of individuals, families, carers, groups and communities to access services;
- challenge their own organisation on behalf of individuals, families, groups and communities;
- challenge injustice and lack of access to services;
- challenge poor practice;
- advise individuals, families, groups and communities about independent advocacy that can meet their needs.

Enable individuals, families, groups and communities to be empowered to represent their views.

Help individuals, families, groups and communities to represent their views in all meetings affecting them.

Involve independent advocates, where appropriate.

This chapter will help you achieve the following key social work benchmarks (Quality Assurance Agency for Higher Education, 2008):

Honours graduates in social work should be able to work effectively with others, i.e. to:

- involve service users to increase their resources, capacity and power to influence factors affecting their lives;
- consult actively with others, including service users and carers, who hold relevant information or expertise;
- act cooperatively with others, liaising and negotiating across differences such as organisational and professional boundaries and differences of identity or language;
- develop effective helping relationships and partnerships with other individuals, groups and organisations that facilitate change;
- act with others to increase social justice by identifying and responding to prejudice, institutional discrimination and structural inequality;
- act within a framework of multiple accountability (for example, to agencies, the public, service users, carers and others);
- challenge others when necessary, in ways that are most likely to produce positive outcomes.

Introduction

In this chapter we will look at the knowledge and skills that underpin the promotion of service user empowerment, participation and advocacy in social work and social care in line with current government policy (e.g. DoH, 2001a, 2001b, 2006). The idea of service user empowerment is seen as central to the values that underpin professionalism in social work and social care, where a strong emphasis is placed on participatory practice and strategies of professional advocacy (Banks, 2006). Putting these values into practice requires both understanding and commitment to move beyond well-meaning sentiment and rhetoric, and it is the aim of this chapter to help develop both.

We will begin by identifying four different models of empowerment. This is necessary in order to develop an understanding of this concept from which we can shape an approach to practice. Although this discussion will be of relevance to all social care client groups, I will focus mainly on working with people with learning difficulties, partly because that is where my own knowledge and experience lie, but also because lessons learned in relation to this particular group can be of universal value when applied to other client groups. People with learning difficulties have historically been among the most disempowered and oppressed social groups in the UK (and many other societies), and their struggle for empowerment is both instructive and inspirational. So let us begin by looking at the concept of empowerment, and examine why it is so important in the social care field.

Empowerment

To understand why empowerment is such an important issue in social work and social care we need to appreciate that the experience of many of its main client groups – people with learning difficulties, people with mental health problems, disabled people and older people, for example – has often been one of extreme disempowerment. The reasons for this are many and varied, but the end result has been a common experience of a devalued identity and social role, and a voice that has rarely been listened to or taken seriously. To explore the impact of this, think about the following.

ACTIVITY **3.1**

Think of an incident or occasion when you had something of great importance that you wanted to say, but you didn't know how to express it, or those with power over you either would not listen or take what you had to say seriously. How did this make you feel?

Comment

Many of us have experiences like this that we can remember – often from childhood. They tend to stay with us for years, often burning and niggling away inside us because of their deep emotional impact. Do you remember perhaps feelings of anger, rage, frustration and a deep sense of injustice?

Now think about what might have happened if this kind of experience had occurred over and over again, perhaps on a daily basis, for most of your life. If for example you had little or no choice over where you live, who with, when and what you eat or drink, how you spend your days, what time you get up, or go to bed, what clothes you wear, etc.

What kind of impact do you think this might have had on your understanding of who you are, how valuable your voice or opinion is, and how you might feel about, and behave towards, those who control your life?

Sadly, we have a very good understanding of the impact of a life lived with this degree of powerlessness because we have frequently seen the effects on people who have been forced to live such lives because the dominant view of powerful professional and social elites has been that they are unable to live any other way. The effects, we know, range from a passive, learned helplessness, to bizarre, disturbed and aggressive forms of challenging behaviour, often directed at themselves or other 'inmates'; all symptomatic of a deeply devalued identity and low self-esteem. There have been many famous studies of oppressive and restrictive regimes in large institutional settings, some of which were highly influential in helping to create the case for deinstitutionalisation and community care (e.g. Goffman, 1961; Wolfensberger, 1975).

The shift towards community-based care in the UK in the 1980s led to a widespread improvement in the standard of services. On its own, however, it failed to address the fundamental imbalance of power between professionals, staff and service users that perpetuates the disempowerment of the latter. It is for this reason that the issue of empowerment is still so important for people who use and rely on social care services, and for those social care professionals and workers who wish to work in ways that liberate, rather than restrict and control, their clients.

Although it is a commonly used term in social work and social care, the concept of empowerment is actually rarely defined. It is, in fact, a contentious idea, with competing models arising from different views about the nature and use of power in society. We will now look at some of these models.

Models of empowerment

In relation to social care four main models and theoretical perspectives have been influential.

The consumerist model

Derived from neo-liberal economic theory, this model sees the problem as a lack of choice in services and support for service users. The solution is seen as using 'market forces' by opening up state-dominated systems to allow more service providers to operate – particularly from the private and voluntary sector – thus, theoretically at least, creating more choice. This model was pursued by Conservative governments in the 1980s and early 1990s in their community care reforms, which introduced a 'market' style system in which a variety of providers would compete to provide the services needed by service-user groups, who were defined as 'consumers'. Since 1997 New Labour governments have adapted this approach further by promoting greater service user control over budgets – via direct payments, for example – which they can then use to buy the services and support they need (Wall and Owen, 2002).

The political model

This model, influenced by neo-Marxist ideas and social movement politics, identifies the problem as oppressive discrimination against marginalised social groups, and the solution is seen as collective action to pursue a rights-based agenda by groups such as the disability movement, the self-advocacy movement for people with learning difficulties, and the survivors' movement for people with mental health problems. A strong influence on this approach has been the social model of disability, a theoretical perspective developed by disabled people in which it is argued that services and professions who work with disabled people often act in an oppressive way in their lives because their understanding of disability comes not from disabled people themselves, but from powerful elites, such as the medical profession. This medical model of disability focuses on pathology in the individual and is consequently preoccupied with the need to diagnose, treat and provide lifelong, medically dominated care. In contrast, the social model redefines disability as a form of oppression imposed on people who experience various kinds of 'impairment', or functional difficulty – physical, sensory or intellectual (Oliver,1996).

The personal/cultural model

This model is influenced by feminist and postmodern ideas, and self-help politics. From this perspective empowerment involves redefining roles, identities and beliefs, as a basis for political and economic action. Strategies involve forming groups and organisations, and/or undertaking cultural activities (including in art, literature, music, etc.) in order for oppressed groups to create their own identity and voice, rather than letting these be created for them by dominant groups and professions. This is a strategy that has also been followed with some success in the disability movement, with some theorists and activists arguing that society in general needs to embrace and celebrate a much wider diversity of human capacity and experience (French and Swain, 2008).

The professional model

This is arguably the most contentious model of all in that it has been argued by some that professionals are part of the problem rather than part of the solution (French and Swain, 2001). Professional models of empowerment have often been based on a 'professional expertise'-led approach which has emphasised getting clients to 'do things for themselves', focusing on issues such as self-care, feeding and mobility, for example. Oliver (1996), however, has pointed out that this is a very limited idea of empowerment. Real empowerment lies, he argues, in giving disabled people legal rights and control of budgets and service systems in order to take control of their lives, including the autonomy to choose where they live, whom they are supported by, and how, when and what type of support is provided. These are strong arguments, but it also needs to be remembered that there is a well-established tradition of professional radicalism which has often been at the forefront of advocating for empowering change (e.g. Wolfensberger, 1972; O'Brien and Tyne, 1981). The model of empowerment put forward by social model theorists like Oliver does, however, challenge the way in which services and support for disabled people have traditionally been provided, and it is a perspective that has gained increasing influence over government policy, which emphasises, for example, increased service-user control over budgets, service commissioning and decision-making processes in social care. Though still in its early stages, this agenda has created a challenge to traditional power relationships in social care, and will inevitably lead to a reshaping of professional roles, identities, knowledge and skills in the process.

This brief review of models of empowerment should provide us with a feel for the ideas that influence thinking and policy in this area. It should be remembered, however, that, in practice, these models are not implemented in a mutually exclusive way. The policy agenda of the New Labour government has, for example, mixed elements from all these models to some extent, although the consumerist model has certainly dominated government thinking since the 1980s.

Implications for practice

We will now look at some of the implications for practice by focusing on strategies to promote service user participation. This discussion will be based on a research summary developed by Sutcliffe and the late, great pioneer of research into the empowerment of people with learning difficulties, Ken Simons (Sutcliffe and Simons, 1995). It thus represents an evidence-based approach to promoting empowerment by encouraging and developing service user participation. It also will form a basis for the identification of key skills areas needed to achieve it.

RESEARCH SUMMARY

Sutcliffe and Simons (1995) identified nine main themes emerging from research into promoting empowerment in practice.

1. **Professionals must be willing to learn from the experience of people with learning difficulties themselves, and their significant others.** *This involves asking ourselves questions about who are the experts, and about what? We have seen above that an important criticism of professional practice from the social model of disability is that it is based on a medically orientated expertise about disability, rather than the lived experience of disabled people themselves. To illustrate this, consider the following activity.*

ACTIVITY 3.2

We know that Down's syndrome is, in the vast majority of cases, caused by an extra chromosome on the 21st pairing – known in genetic jargon as 'trisomy 21'. Now think about what use this knowledge might be, and to whom?

RESEARCH SUMMARY *continued*

Comment

The detection of an extra 21st chromosome in pre-natal screening will tell us that an individual has Down's syndrome, but it will not tell us how severe their level of intellectual impairment will be, or how they will be affected by other characteristics associated with Down's syndrome. These will express themselves in a way unique to that individual, in the same way that they do in all of us, despite our genetic similarity to one another. And their expression will be heavily influenced by the individual's interaction with their family, social and cultural environment – including with health and social care professionals and agencies. What is also missing is the self-knowledge and expertise of people with Down's syndrome themselves – which is actually much more relevant and useful to people with Down's syndrome and their carers in managing their lives on a day-to-day basis. Fortunately, the growth of the self-advocacy movement has allowed this self-knowledge and expertise to become increasingly available (e.g. Souza, with Ramcharan, 1997), and it is up to all professionals, care workers and carers to make sure that they access and use it. Adopting such an approach is central for developing skills in empowering practice. Important skills areas here will include:

- research and networking skills to identify and access sources of service user knowledge and expertise – via the internet, academic library resources and self-help/self-advocacy groups for example, and the growing wealth of literary sources written and informed by disabled people and their allies;

- listening and communicating in ways that allow the voice and perspective of service users to emerge and inform your own, and your organisation's, thinking and practice – valuing this perspective and expertise as much as the 'technical' and theoretical knowledge of human science experts;

- developing a sound understanding of a social model of disability perspective, and working with disabled people to find jointly developed, problem-solving, enabling solutions.

2. **It will take time for staff and people with learning difficulties to develop the necessary skills and confidence.** *People with learning difficulties may require significant amounts of training and personal support to develop the skills and confidence necessary to self-advocate, and/or participate in taking a greater degree of control over their lives. This will take time and require a long-term commitment from individual professionals and their service organisations. This will be shown by placing an emphasis on supporting, rather than controlling, the processes of service user organisation and development, and ensuring that these groups maintain an independent role and identity. Important skill areas involved here will be:*

RESEARCH SUMMARY *continued*

- *negotiation and collaboration with service users' groups and organisations to identify and meet development needs;*
- *promoting the development of a collaborative culture, as outlined below in relation to theme 5.*

3. **The amount of control and autonomy an individual can exercise will vary.** *An important principle in working with people with learning difficulties, and other vulnerable client groups, is the idea of maintaining a 'person-centred' focus (Gates, 2005). This recognises that, whatever 'condition' a person may be affected by, an empowering practice needs to focus on individuals, rather than conditions or 'syndromes'. This is a critical point in promoting respect for individual autonomy that should guide our approach to working with any client, allowing us to recognise and appreciate individual variations in ability and capacity and actual level of involvement. Empowerment is about choice, and that includes the choice not to participate. Even where an individual shows a preference not to be involved in formal processes and procedures of participation, a commitment should still be made to organise their care and support in line with their known wishes and preferences. Key skills areas here will include the following.*

- *The development of person-centred assessment skills that focus on the needs and wishes of individuals. This does not just mean familiarity with forms and procedures, but with the empathic and sensitive communication skills needed to build a trusting relationship with individual service users and/or their carer/advocate.*
- *Developing a commitment to learn about, and disseminate the impact of impairments that affect individuals – and use that to help develop a shared expertise, as described above in relation to theme 1.*
- *Collaboration with 'important others', including informal carers, in the person's life, as well as collaboration with professionals and carers from various services and agencies, such as health and education.*
- *Developing a knowledge of actual and potential sources of help and support – services, professions, agencies, and community resources – to meet your clients' needs, and achieve their desired goals.*

4. **We need to adapt structures, not people.** *Carr (2004), in a review of research into the promotion of service user participation by local authorities in the UK, identified the way that it can be undermined and turned into a tokenistic exercise by organisational failings. Among these are the failure to recognise that promoting empowerment and participation requires organisations to learn how to transform their systems, practices and processes to make them accessible to, and usable for, service user groups and individuals. Key skill areas here involve:*

- *supporting the development of good systems of independent representation for service users – both individually and/or collectively as appropriate – via networking and building relationships with appropriate service user-led organisations;*

- *use of appropriate communication systems and procedures which are 'user friendly', open and accessible to service users, carers and advocates – this includes using plain speech and written language, but also skills in use of signing and/or audio-visual systems.*

5. **We need to change the culture** *from one where we talk about people to one where we talk in dialogue with them about their lives and aspirations. In their research-based approach to promoting service user participation, Beresford and Trevillion (1995) emphasised the importance of creating a collaborative culture in care and support services. At the core of this lie communication skills that help to develop trust and good relationships between professionals, staff and service users themselves, and also their families, relatives and other carers (see Chapters 1 and 2). In particular, they place commitment to the involvement of service users at the centre of their strategy for creating a collaborative culture and practice. Key skill areas they specify are:*

- *allowing space and time for involvement, at whatever level the service user is able or willing to be involved;*

- *a commitment to including the service user, their advocate or representative in decision-making at all levels, including important life choices;*

- *keeping the use of technical language in its appropriate context;*

- *not sacrificing service-user interests to inter-professional power play or disputes, and to be led by the needs of the service user, and keeping areas of potential conflict – such as what constitutes a 'health' rather than a 'social' care need – out of meetings involving the service user or their supporters, for example.*

These points echo many of those made previously, and we can see that communication systems and skills are at the heart of promoting service user empowerment and participation. But the core point to emphasise once again here is the idea of care and support based on an ongoing dialogue, and the development of a shared expertise, on a person-by-person basis.

6. **We need to celebrate diversity in people and solutions to their problems.** *A dialogue-based, person-centred approach, as advocated by Gates (2005) for example, to providing care and support will inevitably move us away from the kind of 'one-size-fits-all', resource-led solutions which have tended to dominate service delivery in the past. An approach that emphasises using dialogue with individual service users and/or their representatives to identify their needs and aspirations, and the problems they face in meeting and achieving them is central. In addition to skill areas already identified, an important area here is:*

- *the development of creative problem-solving skills – where problems are seen not as insurmountable barriers but as challenges to be overcome by mobilising the shared expertise of yourself, the service user, and their supporters and allies.*

7. **We need to face up to tensions over who speaks for whom, and recognise that different stakeholders (service users, informal carers, staff and professionals) have different agendas.** *For people with intellectual disabilities in particular – learning difficulties, brain damage, stroke, dementia – the issue of whose voice is dominant is often crucial in deciding the extent to which their wishes, desires and preferences are met in designing and delivering care and support – particularly if that person has either never developed, or lost, their actual voice. For people in this situation the presence of others who can speak for and advocate for them is vital. This role is often taken up automatically by parents and/or other relatives – or, where these are absent, or not accessible on a day-today-basis, the care staff or professionals that work with them. It is important to remember that each of these stakeholders has interests that are different and distinct from the individual service user themselves, however. Service staff and professionals may have an interest in making sure that the person continues to use their service, for example, thus perpetuating their employment. Likewise, parents may take a very different view from the young man or woman themselves about whether their young adult son or daughter with a learning difficulty should be allowed to enter into a sexual relationship. These examples illustrate some potential areas of conflict that may have to be faced up to. We shall look at this issue further when we discuss advocacy.*

8. **We need to put service users at the centre** *of our thinking, processes and actions. A person-centred approach to working with service users will necessarily mean that we focus on promoting the needs, desires and aspirations of the person themselves. Care systems are often organised around standard processes and procedures, which can be useful in helping to make sure that systems are effective and efficient. It can also, however, lead us down the procedural path of seeing service users purely as 'cases' to be dealt with, drawing us away from seeing them as individuals with their own life history and story, of which we are only a part. A key skill area here will involve:*

   • *building a warm, human relationship with service users, which will help us to ensure that our thinking and actions stay focused on their needs, rather than ours.*

9. **We need to accept and actively promote the idea that service user led organisations can represent** *the people we support. The research referred to by Carr (2004) reminds us that, for empowerment and participation to be effective rather than tokenistic, we need to address the issue of representation. The self-advocacy movement for people with learning difficulties, like the survivors' movement for people with mental health problems, and the wider disability movement, have all identified the need for collective representation in order to give weight and strength to their voice. This kind of representation can be seen as threatening by service organisations, staff and professionals, however, who have become adept at 'disarming' or ignoring it. Adopting a person-centred service is not a substitute for independent and/or group representation. Instead such strategies disempower the service user by denying them the right to involvement in the development of an*

independent, collective voice. It takes great courage and tenacity to take on en-trenched professional and organisational power, and even more so if you lack the confidence, knowledge and skills necessary. This is what collective representation provides, and history has shown that it is an important part of the struggle of any oppressed group in gaining empowerment. This last point brings us into the realm of advocacy and it is this as a strategy for empowerment which we will look at next.

Advocacy

Advocacy is about speaking up for yourself, or others. The concept of advocacy has its origins in the legal system, and in Western societies there is a strong tradition of professionalised legal advocacy. This is a very powerful and high-profile form of advo-cacy, but it is only one kind. The other main forms include the following.

- **Political advocacy** This includes the rights-based advocacy of the 'disability movement', which focuses mainly on campaigning and lobbying activity.

- **Self-advocacy** This has some cross-over with political advocacy, but centres spe-cifically on service users speaking up for themselves, either individually or collec-tively, and at all levels, from major political issues to day-to-day choices about their lives.

- **Citizen advocacy** This is where a person independent from services takes on the role of speaking up for the interests of the person.

- **Issue advocacy** This is similar to, and perhaps involves, legal advocacy, where trained advocates will take on specific issues for an individual or groups of service users as they arise (Gray and Jackson, 1998).

- **Professional advocacy** This is where a service professional, such as a nurse or social worker, takes on the advocacy role. This can be an important and vital role, although it does have its dangers too, and it is important to remember that effective advocacy may require the absence rather than the intervention of profes-sionals, no matter how well meaning. A social worker, for example, is, inevitably, a representative of the local authority, private or voluntary sector organisation they work for. These are 'interests' that can potentially conflict with those of service users. For example, the organisation may be under pressure to reduce costs, which may lead to pressure to restrict spending to meeting only those needs regarded as essential rather than desirable. Views on what is regarded as essential and desir-able may well vary, however, depending on the perspective of different stake-holders. The first stage of planning any advocacy intervention therefore is to ask the question *am I the right person to do it?* A person-centred focus may require us to accept that our client's interests are better served by an advocate who is inde-pendent of organisational and professional interests that may constrain us – a 'citizen' or 'issue' advocate, for example. This is illustrated further in the following case study.

Angela

Angela is 45 years old. For 20 years she lived in an NHS mental subnormality hospital where she was admitted at the age of 5. She then spent a further 20 years in a number of NHS, social service and private-sector residential homes for people with learning diffi-culties and challenging behaviours. She has a mild learning difficulty, can read and write, is quite articulate and physically able, if overweight. She frequently flew into rages, crying out for her father, who died when she was young (it was his death that led to her admission to hospital), and her mother, with whom she had infrequent telephone contact. She was prescribed antipsychotic medication and antidepressants, and was put on repeated behavioural programmes to help control her temper. When calm and lucid, Angela repeatedly expressed her desire to live on her own, near enough to her mother to visit, get a job and look after herself.

The big change for Angela came when a community learning disability nurse working with her advocated successfully to her service manager that Angela's behaviour should be seen as communicative rather than psychotic. The nurse contacted a social worker, who undertook an assessment which led to a plan being agreed to move Angela to a half-way home where she would learn the skills to help her live independently. There was still some resistance from her psychiatrist and from the owners of the privately run home where she lived, however. To strengthen the case the social worker referred Angela to a local independent advocacy organisation. They appointed an advocate who took up, and successfully argued, Angela's case to live independently, with an appropriate support package from a local housing association.

Angela spent three months in a half-way house, finally moving out of residential care alto-gether. She has now been living independently, with support, for two years. She has a part-time job at a local Co-op, regularly visits her mother who lives within walking distance, and has joined a local self-advocacy group, who also run a variety of social activities, as well as helping Angela gain the knowledge and confidence to speak up for herself.

Comment

We can see that various forms of advocacy played a crucial part in the success of Angela's move from a restricted life, organised and run for her by professional experts, to a life of supported independence, where she earns her own living, has contact with her family, and has her own circle of friends and support. First there was the learning disability nurse, who was able to understand the communicative rather than psychotic nature of her behaviour. She was able to present an evidence-based case to key decision-makers, and collaborate with a social worker who was able to assess Angela's needs and advocate further for a change of approach. Crucially, Angela's social work-er was able to appreciate his own limitations, and involved independent advocates who were able to make the final case to develop a new support package for Angela.

They did not stop there, however, realising that, for Angela to achieve real empowerment in her life she needed help from a self-advocacy organisation that can encourage her to achieve further autonomy.

We are not arguing then that a professional cannot advocate for the interests of his or her clients, and this is, in fact, a key part of the role. In most cases, however, professional advocacy is probably best restricted to service level advocacy – that is, advocating for access to the skills and expertise of other professionals within or across different services. This requires a good level of knowledge about other professional roles, referral systems, finance issues, and about one's own position within the service context, combined with an informed and up-to-date knowledge of interventions and services which may help service users to meet their assessed needs. Key skills will involve preparation and presentation of this case to the appropriate forum. This last point shifts our focus back onto the skills required to promote empowerment, participation and advocacy, and it is that on which we now focus.

Skills for promoting empowerment, participation and advocacy

We have already identified that the key skills areas for promoting empowerment, participation and advocacy centre on communication. Service-user focused communication skills then are at the heart of empowering practice. To summarise, these skills include the following.

- **Assertiveness skills** These include the ability to be able to express your own point of view or perspective in a way that is perceived by others as confident, rather than as passive and/or aggressive. This requires the development of good self-awareness, including awareness of body posture, use of appropriate language, and the ability to listen actively, take on and assimilate the views and perspectives of others. It also involves knowing your limits – being confident enough to say *I don't know*, avoiding the use of technical/professional language wherever possible, using an explanatory communication style, and staying focused on finding solutions (see Chapters 1 and 2).

- **Negotiation skills** Social work often involves negotiating who will do what, how, by when, and who will pay for it. This requires the ability to recognise and head off potential points of conflict, and to resolve them effectively where they do arise. It is important to avoid entering into negotiation with the idea that one party will 'win' and the other will 'lose'. Instead, a problem-solving approach should be used, focusing on meeting the needs and aspiration of service users. Skills relating to both assertiveness and advocacy may come into play here, but negotiation processes will be made a great deal easier if there is a good level of trust and mutual respect to begin with. Time spent establishing good lines of communication and building a good rapport – visiting, introducing oneself, outlining your own role and perspective, establishing a 'common cause' by emphasising your commitment to a user-focused approach – are all important (see Chapter 7).

- **Acting and working in a business-like manner** All of the above will be greatly helped if your own approach is grounded in behaviours associated with professionalism. Reliability, punctuality, and willing participation in operational processes of delegation and workload division will all contribute to demonstrating your commitment to making service–user-focused collaboration work (see Chapters 6, 9 and 11).

- **Encouraging information gathering and sharing** Control of information and its dissemination is one of the ways in which professions have sometimes engaged in oppressive and disempowering practices. The development of a collaborative culture requires a commitment to ensuring that accurate information is gathered and shared at the right time, the right place, and in the right format, primarily with service users, but also those people who need to know how to achieve the best outcomes for service users. The need to protect sensitive information in line with legal and ethical requirements is vital. Key skills in this area involve verbal, written and electronic presentation, together with the use of computer and information technology (see Chapter 8). It may also require the use of alternative and/ or 'augmented' communication systems, the accessing of which may be a number one priority for service users with communication difficulties.

- **Constructive advice, supervision and reflection** Working in social work can be complex and demanding, and good support, supervision and governance systems are important to make it function successfully. The skills of advising, supervising and mentoring staff and other team members are increasingly important. It is also important to ensure that you receive good supervision and mentoring support – particularly if you are to remain reflective about and committed to empowering practice. Joint and collaborative forums for inter-professional discussion and reflection are a useful way of sharing information and knowledge about one another's perspectives, skills and practice, and an opportunity to develop a sense of shared commitment to user-focused methods and approaches to meeting client needs (see Chapter 11).

C H A P T E R   S U M M A R Y

In this chapter we have looked at the knowledge and skills that underpin the promotion of service user empowerment, participation and advocacy in social work and social care. We have explored the idea of service user empowerment and located it in relation to the values that underpin professionalism in social work and social care. We have seen that putting these values into practice requires understanding and commitment, and we have looked at different models of empowerment and the theoretical perspectives that influence them.

We then discussed lessons drawn from research about the strategies and skills required to put our understanding of empowerment and participation into practice, before going on to look specifically at advocacy as a strategy to achieve both. The central message is that we need to develop a 'shared expertise' with service users, based on a dialogue with them about their needs, desires and aspirations, and that we should always strive to ensure we work in ways which promote, rather than hinder, their struggle for empowerment.

Swain, J and French, S (2008) *Disability on equal terms.* London: Sage.
This provides a very good outline of current issues and debates around the empowerment of disabled people, including a very good section on professional practice, with a chapter by Maureen Gill specifically aimed at social workers.

Gray, B and Jackson, R (eds) (2002) *Advocacy and learning disability.* London: Jessica Kingsley.
A useful reader on a variety of issues relating to advocacy.

Beresford, P and Croft, S (2000) User involvement. In Davies, M (ed.) *The Blackwell encyclopedia of social work.* Oxford: Blackwell.
Peter Beresford is a leading figure in research and debates about service user involvement and participation.

Some useful websites on service user participation include:

www.scie-socialcareonline.org.uk
www.serviceuserinvolvement.co.uk
For advocacy see:
www.bild.org.uk
www.peoplefirstltd.com

PART 2
INTERVENING WITH ADULT SERVICE USERS

Chapter 4

Assessing adults
David Gaylard

A C H I E V I N G   A   S O C I A L   W O R K   D E G R E E

This chapter will help you to meet the following National Occupational Standards:

Key Role 1: Prepare for, and work with individuals, families, carers, groups and communities to assess their needs and circumstances.

- Prepare for social work contact and involvement.
- Work with individuals, families, carers, groups and communities to help them make informed decisions.
- Assess the needs and options to recommend a course of action.

Key Role 2: Plan, carry out, review and evaluate social work practice, with individuals, families, carers, groups, communities and other professionals.

- Respond to crisis situations.
- Interact with individuals, families, carers, groups and communities to achieve and develop and improve life opportunities.
- Prepare, produce, implement and evaluate plans with individuals, families, carers, groups, communities and professional colleagues.
- Address behaviour which presents a risk to individuals, families, carers, groups and communities.

Key Role 4: Manage risk to individuals, families, carers, groups, communities, self and colleagues.

- Assess and manage risks to individuals, families, carers, groups and communities.
- Assess, minimise and manage risk to self and colleagues.

Introduction

This chapter aims to explore assessments, one of the primary activities of social work with adults. It will critically examine what we mean by assessment and what is involved in the assessment process. Important practice considerations and service users' and carers' perspectives will also be highlighted. The chapter concludes with a discussion around risk assessment supported by key principles and practice frameworks aimed at enhancing practice and outcomes.

Based upon my experiences as a practice teacher, team manager and tutor, I have noticed that students and practitioners can easily become distracted by the paperwork involved in the assessment process. While this is an appropriate learning objective which can provide a tangible contextual framework, it may produce an assumption of the assessement process as being primarily a bureaucratic one. There are dangerous practice implications in becoming solely dependent upon the actual paperwork process for making a sound assessment. However, the elements of an assessment also involve the skilled application of fundamental values of good listening, honesty, trust, senstivity and empathy (see Chapter 1). A sense of proportionality and a non-judgmental approach are also vital elements of the decision-making process inherent within assessments (see Chapter 5).

Assessments do not happen in a vacuum and the ability to conduct assessments requires not only knowledge about the assessement process, but also the ability and professional confidence to draw upon a broader repertoire of social work skills and social science knowledge. This includes knowledge about particular user groups and social problems, skills pertaining to related research, critical thinking and interviewing, cultural diversity and sensitivity. Social workers must also adhere to the profession's fundamental principles and values underpinned by the GSCC Codes of Conduct and the BASW Code of Ethics (2002). You will also need to have a clear understanding of the concerns and restraints upon the other professions with whom you work.

Crucially, assessments require you to gather and analyse information from differing and sometimes competing perspectives. This process is undertaken within the context of recognising your legislative duties and powers, while steering between the competing pressures of organisational demands, limited rescources, risk, choice and personal agendas.

What is an assessment?

Assessments are an ongoing process, in which the users or carers participate, whose purpose is to understand people in relation to their environment; it is a basis for planning what needs to be done to maintain, improve or bring about change in the person, the person's environment or both.

(Coulshed and Orme, 2006, p29)

It is important to differentiate between carers' and service users' needs and how they are currently met. For example, a woman who has suffered an acquired brain injury and who can exhibit aggressive behaviour may present as having no needs on a specialist behavioural ward. However, placed in her own home she may be at significant risk to herself and others.

Social workers currently undertake a wide range of assessments within the field of adult work, for example, adult safeguard investigations, mental health assessments (under the Mental Health Act 2007), Community Care assessment (s. 47 NHS and Community Care Act 1990), specific assessments for carers (Carers [Recognition and Services] Act 1995). Often these assessments may share common themes.

- Establishing a need – This can help to highlight what needs to change. This may be considered differently by the carer, the service user and the social worker.

- Eligibility for services – Identifying what needs to change does not necessarily mean that you are the right person to meet that need. Sometimes just through clarifying their concerns a person may be empowered to manage their difficulties. In other cases it may be that they require a different or more specialist service. Assessment is used as a tool by agencies to provide fair access to resources according to need. However, often in adult services eligibility criteria has been about gatekeeping limited resources, e.g. Fair Access to Care eligibility thresholds.

- Risk assessment – This often requires assessment of a person's capacity in order to balance advocacy and empowerment with duties to protect (see below).

- Determining the effectiveness of services provided or the suitability of other service providers.

Consequently it is important to know why you are undertaking an assessment. For example, always have a clear understanding of your role and purpose in assessment work. Know the reason why your agency is undertaking an assessment: to what purpose may or will an assessment be used? Try to plan ahead carefully for all assessment work. Be mindful of your power (be it perceived or real) as a social worker in an assessment role and always adhere to anti-oppressive practice principles.

Assessment begins from the first point of contact (which may not always be 'face to face') and may be a relatively short, simple process or more complex one involving a number of people over an extended period of time. It is important to remember that carers and people who use services are assessing us at the same time, determining how credible they consider us to be and consequently impacting on our own assessment.

Situations do not remain static; consequently assessments are a fluid and dynamic process which involve investigative, preventative and negotiative elements (see Chapter 7), while trying to sustain a collaborative basis.

Adult social care law policy and guidance: a need for reform?

Adult social care law has been dominated by piecemeal development. This evolutionary process has resulted in overlapping and conflicting obligations, for example, traditional service-led provision, carers' assessments and self-directed support. The last 60 years of social policy have witnessed rapid and fundamental changes, in terms of demographic trends, expectations and demand for social care. The scope of some of this legislation now encompasses outdated definitions, language and concepts. The main objectives of adult social care law reform are to provide a clearer, more coherent legal framework through simplification, consistency and transparency for practitioners, service users and carers. However, it aims to be 'resource neutral', while embracing modern 21st century consumerist expectations of social care provision.

At the time of writing, the Law Commission (an independent body responsible for the development of law reform in England and Wales) is advocating adult social care law reform. At the end of 2008, the Commission completed the first stage of a three-staged review process of adult social care law by completing a scoping review to identify areas for reform. The Law Commission now intends to publish a consultation reform paper, and to undertake a broad consultation on proposals during 2010, before publishing a report with reform recommendations in 2011 in preparation for a draft bill by 2012.

Why are assessments important?

Assessments remain a key task in social work practice. Public inquiries have focused on the importance placed upon judgments and assessments undertaken by social workers. The importance of good social work assessment has been particuarly emphasised in child abuse inquiries, such as the Victoria Climbié Inquiry (Laming, 2003), and more recently with regard to Baby 'P', which are equally relevant to adult social work. Public inquiries resulted in stronger emphasis and importance being placed upon risk in order to predict, minimise or intervene. Reports have also identified the need for social workers to have the professional confidence to question other agencies in their involvement and conclusions (Rec. 37 Victoria Climbié Inquiry, Laming, 2003).

A thorough 'holistic assessment' is crucial to the success of social work interventions. Extra time taken in the initial assessment can save substantial amounts of time later and ensure that scarce resources and carer and service user goodwill are not wasted.

Assessment concerns

Undertaking something new or starting a task for the first time is often challenging and can generate some level of anxiety or doubt. Wilson, et al. (2008, p268) provide a useful summary of key concerns for practitioners:

- *What am I trying to achieve and where do I begin?*
- *What information is pertinent, why and according to whom?*
- *Whose views do I incorporate?*
- *How do I make sense of, interpret and most accurately record and represent the information I have gathered?*

ACTIVITY *4.1*

ACTIVITY 4.1

Try to identify and reflect upon a situation in which you have been assessed.

• *What did the process involve?*

• *What did you feel about this experience?*

• *What characteristics or skills adopted by the assessor facilitated or hindered the process?*

Comment

You may have found that you were unclear about what was expected of you and what the criteria for the assessment were. This can leave you feeling frustrated and powerless. Clear and concise assessments enable practitioners and potential service users to share a sound understanding of the purpose, process, nature and extent of professional involvement. Wilson et al. (2008) highlight that good beginnings, in particular, are an essential component of effective professional practice, setting the tone for future interventions.

What does an assessment involve?

Assessment involves a range of activities in which social workers, service users and carers describe, explain, predict, evaluate, and prescribe. Smale and Tuson (1993) identified three different models of assessment which are closely linked to social work in terms of risk, resources and needs factors.

The questioning model

The worker holds the expertise, follows a format of questions, listens to and processes the answers. This process reflects the social worker's agenda in which the data are shaped to fit the social worker's theories about the nature of people, for example, a psychodynamic approach.

The procedural model

In this, the social worker fulfils the agency's functions by gathering information to see whether the subject 'fits' criteria for services. Little judgment is required; checklists may also be used, for example, care management.

The exchange model

All users are viewed as 'experts' on their own problems, so emphasis is placed on exchanging information. The social worker follows or 'tracks' what other people are saying rather than interpreting what they think is meant. The practitioner then works in partnership to identify how the service user can mobilise their internal and external resources in order to reach goals defined by the service user on their terms, for example, solution-focused approaches.

ACTIVITY 4.2

Which model do you tend to use?
Which model do you feel more comfortable working with, and why?

Comment

The exchange model is often perceived as the most desirable model of choice. Routine service-led assessments are the antithesis of an empowering approach to assessment and care management (Smale, 1994). The exchange model comes nearest to meeting a needs-led assessment. It embraces principles outlined in current government guidance and has potential to lead to re-evaluation. A questioning model is most likely to be used when risk factors provide the emphasis of the assessment. The procedural model fits assessment subject to resource constraints. The questioning and procedural models are often found in combination. Professional tensions will always exist when demand for resources exceeds supply, resulting in needs-led versus resource-led assessments. What happens to those who fail to qualify, or do not know how to access or utilise the system to their advantage? Or those who do not have critical or substantial assessed need? What happened to preventative work?

Balancing needs involves making well-informed, evidence-based decisions and often hard choices about who gets a service at a given moment and who does not. This operates within resource-allocation panel meetings chaired by team or senior managers. Within most public services there is typically a division of responsibility between practitioners, who assess needs, and managers, who make decisions about how resources should be allocated.

Often practitioners tend to blame managers for not making resources available. Managers in turn may disassociate themselves from day-to-day contact with human distress and so blame practitioners for casework that goes wrong. This split of responsibilities is not necessarily the most healthy as a too rigid split between 'practice' and 'resource' decisions ignores the fact that they are closely intertwined (Walker and Beckett, 2003). The Laming Inquiry (2003) criticised senior managers for considering themselves *not responsible for the day to day realities*. This is equally relevant to social work that operates within an adult social care context. Practitioners collect the assessment information that managers use to make decisions about priorities, and so are implicated in those decisions. Managers who allocate work and inadequate resources must also share the responsibility in the success or failure of that undertaking. In reality social care staff at all levels have to think not only about what is desirable in an ideal world but also what is possible to do in the real world (Beckett and Maynard, 2006).

Theory into practice

> *Assessment has been recognised as a core skill in social work and should underpin interventions, there is no singular theory or understanding as to what the purpose of assessment is and what the process should entail.*
>
> (Crisp, et al., 2003, p1)

Learning by doing is an essential component in the development of your assessment skills and has long been a hallmark of social work training. Students and practitioners require opportunities to continually refine and develop key assessment skills. This necessitates drawing upon the range of theories and synthesising them into your practice. It also requires that you are a creative lateral thinker in terms of finding ways to meaningfully involve users and carers in all stages of an assessment process. For example, networking skills are crucial.

While assessing others you also assess your own development through feedback from carers, people who use services, colleagues, supervision and self-reflection (see Chapters 10 and 11).

Working with people, not problems

It is important to be aware of not becoming preoccupied with a problem. Assessments involve being an effective listener, but if we are focused on a particular issue we may miss other important information or in our questioning we may not provide the individual with the oportunity to raise possibly more significant issues. Such a focus can also obscure an individual's strengths and resources and promote learned helpnessness. In extreme situations this can lead to pathologising service users. We must remember that the person is not the problem: 'the problem is the problem'. Remaining solution-focused can motivate and build service users' confidence, empowering people to find their own answers. During assessments try to seek evidence from service users in terms of inner personal strengths, talents, past achievements, future possibilities, level of potential resources and competence.

CASE STUDY

Sally is a young parent who has been seen shouting loudly at her children and becoming frustrated and angry with them, causing concern about her parenting capacity. How would you initially respond to Sally if you adopted a solution-focused approach?

Comment

As practitioners we do need to listen, as this affects what we actually ask. There is a tendency to ask problem-focused questions; however, if we adopt a solution-focused approach we can listen for evidence of exceptions, strengths and successes in terms of an individual's competencies, resources and achievements. So for example, when working with Sally you could ask her about those times when she would have usually shouted but did not. Was Sally able to recall a recent occasion when she had spoken calmly to her children because (say, in the supermarket) she did not want to be embarrassed in public? Ask her how she did that. Sally may be able to recall that she took some deep breaths and thought about the nice times she had with her children. This may enable Sally to think about how she could use similar techniques in the future, providing her with ways of dealing with her children that enhance her existing skills and develop her personal agency. Rather than imposing a set of externally constructed parenting skills, Sally would be able to recognise and draw upon her personal experiences to plot her own course to deal with the problem, using the exceptions to follow her easiest path to a problem-free future (Dolan, 1991).

Sensitive information gathering

ACTIVITY **4.3**

Imagine you are going through airport security and the staff examine the contents of your bags.
How would you feel?
Would it matter if they were a different gender or age to you?

Comment

You might feel it is just a normal part of the process for boarding a plane, but it is more likely that you will feel embarrassed and find the process intrusive. Yet this intrusion into your privacy is minor compared with our own incursions into people's lives. It is easy to become blasé and desensitised to the enormity of what we ask of others when we undertake an assessment. By the very nature of social work with adults, our clients are often dealing with loss of independence or trauma which they have yet to process. Yet we expect them to openly discuss their concerns with us.

It is, therefore, always essential to be sensitive to carers and service users during assessments. This includes respecting inner abilities and protective strategies. A wealthy woman with multiple sclerosis once recounted to me that after carrying out an assessment of her and her husband, the social worker summarised their situation by saying that they were like two birds in a gilded cage. She said that she was devastated by this comment; it had really brought home to her how she felt trapped within her house.

Always check your assessment carefully with users and carers for historical accuracy and with others contributing to the process. Treat the information you have gained with the utmost care and sensitivity and let them know the bounds and limits of confidentiality. It is also essential to know the Freedom of Information Act 2000 in relation to the public's right to access information held by public authorities (Parker and Bradley, 2007).

The perspectives of service users on assessments

Most carers or people who use services seek help in relation to themselves or others, their current living situation or wider social network for three main reasons, namely:

- to help/support individuals to maintain the quality of life they currently have and avoid deterioration;

- to help/support individuals to introduce/consider limited changes (where the system itself remains unchanged);

- to help/support individuals to introduce/consider more radical change(s) (where changes occur in the system itself).

(Trevithick, 2006, pp126–7)

Assessment outcomes may ultimately result in greater independence and control, and improve quality of life through sensitive service provision, for example, self-directed support or direct payment schemes. However, the assessment process can often be experienced as intrusive and disempowering. The following factors, in particular, can inhibit user empowerment.

- The statutory agency often retains power over the allocation of resources.

- Users often become overwhelmed by the number of professionals involved.

- The concept of 'assessed needs' rather than individual rights may itself be disabling.

- Assessment can raise users' expectations of choice, which statutory agencies are often unable to deliver on economic or principled rationing grounds.

(Griggs, 2000)

The simple provision of information can at times empower people to make choices, but people often need support to understand and negotiate the health and social care system. Practitioners need to consider what impairments may affect communication and the level of understanding of people who use services (see Chapters 1 and 2). In some situations social workers need to consider whether advocates should also be involved in the assessment (see Chapter 3).

Assessment skills identified by service users

Feedback from both children and adult service users identified the following skills: to be listened to; for practitioners to be available and accessible; to be non-judgmental and non-directive (for example, anti-oppressive or anti-discriminatory practice). Practitioners needed to have a sense of humour and be honest and 'straight-talking', for example, the use of 'jargon-free' language with no abbreviations. Service users wanted to be able to trust practitioners and, where appropriate, to have confidentiality respected. Confidentiality issues should be highlighted at the outset of the assessment process and not left until matters arise. Users fully appreciated and understood that it was not always possible for all information to be kept confidential (Dept of Education and Employment, 2000).

One of the most contentious areas of social work practice with adults is the balance between advocacy and protection. While this decision should rest fundamentally on the assessment of their capacity to make their own decisions, risk assessments are necessary to clarify the level of risk and identify appropriate levels of intervention. This tension can become more challenging when working within multi-disciplinary contexts (see Chapter 6) as related health and social care professionals tend to hold differing views regarding thresholds and perceptions of risk.

RESEARCH SUMMARY

Living with risk
Langan and Lindow (2004) examined risk assessment and risk management for people being discharged from psychiatric hospitals into the community. Langan and Lindow specifically asked users about their views on and experiences of posing a former or potential risk to other people. Their findings indicated that the stigma associated with risk had caused users distress in terms of their personal safety, which led to occasional disengagement from services. Service users felt that practice around risk assessment was inconsistent: agreements between service users and professionals with regards to levels of risk were extremely variable. Recorded information kept on files was found to be inaccurate and had omissions to the point that it put the service users at risk.

Assessment of risk

Undertaking risk assessments can generate anxiety, uncertainty and fear of 'getting it wrong'. Based upon my experiences as a practitioner, there has been a tendency for social care organisations to issue procedural remedies in the form of 'tick box' risk-assessment tools which aim to aid practitioners in the field. Although these tools may initially appear reassuring for practitioners, they pose a real danger to the development of defensive practice. By ascribing risk labels to people, practitioners can potentially lose sight of the individual, perpetuating unethical and oppressive practice.

What do we mean by risk?

Social workers frequently struggle with the notion of risk, risk assessment and management, often confusing these different terms.

- Risk is the likelihood of an event happening with potentially harmful (or sometimes beneficial) outcomes for self and others. Possible behaviours may include falls, suicide, self-harm, aggression or violence.

- Risk assessment can be defined as the gathering of information through processes of communication, investigation and observation; and the analysis of the potential outcomes of identified behaviours, identifying specific risk factors of relevance to an individual and the circumstances in which they occur. This process requires linking the context of historical information to current circumstances, to anticipate possible future change.

- Risk management is the statement of plans and allocation of responsibilities for translating collective decisions into real actions; an activity of exercising a duty of care where risks (both positive and negative) are identified. Activities may involve preventative, responsive and supportive measures to diminish the potential negative consequences of risk and to promote potential benefits of taking appropriate risk. Dates should be clearly identified for reviewing the assessment and management plans.

- Positive risk-taking is weighing up the potential benefits and harms of exercising one choice of action over another, identifying the risk involved and developing plans and actions that reflect the positive capabilities and stated priorities of service users. It involves using available resources and support to achieve the desired outcomes while minimising any possible harmful outcomes. It involves clear explanations of goals, and any differences of opinion regarding ownership, goals or courses of action.   (adapted from Morgan, 2000)

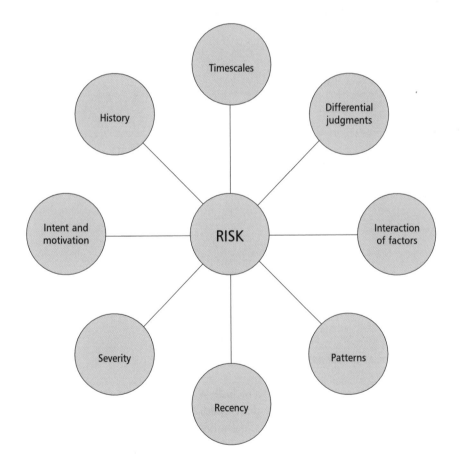

Figure 4.1 Components of risk

It is important to approach any risk in a planned and structured way. Figure 4.1 outlines the main components to consider when undertaking a risk assessment. History can sometimes be a guide to future behaviour (but not always). Sometimes patterns of risk or risk triggers can be repeated. The more recent a pattern of risk, the more likely it is to recur, but this does not mean it will occur. The degree of severity should inform your assessment. An individual's intent and motivation is another variable to take into account. The interaction of risk factors may be dependent upon one key variable, for example, alcohol or substance misuse.

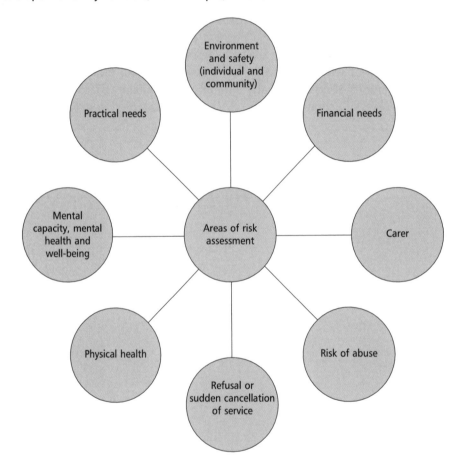

Figure 4.2 Key areas of risk assessment

Figure 4.2 highlights common areas to include within a risk assessment. When a risk is identified, key strategies need to be developed around the importance of recording and ensuring your manager and key stakeholders remain informed.

The serious case and internal management review undertaken by Cornwall Social Services Department, published in December 2007, following the murder of Steve Hoskin, crucially highlighted that Steve Hoskin's decision to end contact with social services had not been reviewed, investigated or risk-assessed. Pivotal in addressing risk is the integral involvement of users and carers in the decision-taking and effective sharing and co-ordination of information with others.

Prioritising risk

Indicators of risk can be weighed into three main categories which will identify the degree, severity and urgency of responses needed. If risk is addressed and managed effectively, this in turn minimises potential harm to oneself and others. Variables that need to be taken into consideration when measuring risk are:

- physical capability of the user;
- mental capacity of the user;
- environment: is it safe for both the user and carers?;
- action already taken to reduce risk.

Social care organisations have created systems to prioritise risk into three categories: critical or high (for example, actual or imminent harm), medium (for example, likelihood of harm if action not taken) and low (for example, potential risk of harm – a gradual deterioration of situation if risk is not addressed). This provides a conceptual framework which gives practitioners, users, carers and organisations a level of indication in terms of the severity of risk and the urgency of response required. This has led to a growth in providing practitioners with clear guidelines on their responsibilities to minimise potential risk to users or carers.

Assessing risk: The seven-stage approach

- Stage 1: For whom is the risk involved? The referrer; the assessor; the service user; the carer; the wider community?
- Stage 2: Is the risk chosen, welcomed, imposed or resented?
- Stage 3: What is the nature of the risk? Physical, sexual, psychological/emotional, discriminatory, institutional, inter-personal, financial, neglect or a combination.
- Stage 4: What are the likelihoods of the risk occurring on a scale between minimal and inevitable?
- Stage 5: What options are available in relation in the risk? Taking the risk or not taking the risk? Are the options proportionate to the actual level of risk? What alternative courses of action could be considered?.
- Stage 6: What values are attached to each option? If positive – how important? If negative – how serious?
- Stage 7: In light of the above, what is the balance for and against the risk being taken?

(Adapted from Royal Borough of Kensington and Chelsea, 2000)

Comment

This seven-stage approach to assessing risk may appear complex but aims to clarify practitioners' thinking by raising the fundamental questions that need to be explored. This will ensure that an assessment of risk remains thorough, while trying to remain proportionate in terms of an individual's capacity, independence, choices, well-being, activities of daily living and personal liberty.

Key practice principles for working with risk

Risk remains dynamic, constantly changing in response to altered circumstances. Remember that everyday activities of life will continue to involve some element of risk (for example, crossing a road); therefore, risk can only be minimised not completely eliminated. Risk assessments can be enhanced by multiple sources of information but frequently as practitioners you may well be working with incomplete, partial or inaccurate data at the time. The assessment of information and subsequent decision-making can be improved by engaging multi-agency collaboration through discussions and joint care planning, involving users and carers as much as possible.

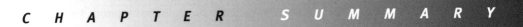

C H A P T E R   S U M M A R Y

As we have seen, assessments are one of the primary roles of social work activity within adult social care. Assessments do not occur in a vacuum and the ability to conduct assessments not only requires knowledge about the assessment process, but also the ability and professional confidence to draw upon a broader repertoire of social work skills and social science knowledge. User involvement remains central to the concept of community care assessments so practitioners need to continue to strive to empower users to fully participate in the assessment process. With the rapid expansion of personalisation across adult social care, users are now in a position to self-assess their own needs but sometimes may be reluctant to take part in the assessment process due to a life crisis point, so may still require sensitive guidance, assistance and direction. However, assessments will remain crucial to social care delivery and will continue to be used by a variety of statutory and voluntary social care agencies to provide fair access to resources.

In addition, the assessment of risk has also been a central theme in the assessment of need, so managing risk remains an inherent social work activity within statutory adult social care. In assessing risk, practitioners need to carry out a holistic and thorough assessment that incorporates information from users and carers, relatives, friends, independent care providers, advocates and any other key professionals.

FURTHER READING

Cree, V and Myers, S (2008) *Social work: Making a difference*. Bristol: Policy Press.
A well-researched text, structured around the six National Occupational Standards, with comprehensive problem-based scenarios supported by good links to legislation, policy and underpinning values aiding reflective learning and effective practice.

Myers, S (2008) *Solution-focused approaches*. Lyme Regis: Russell House.
This is an accessible introductory text which covers both theory and practice for those who wish to learn more about solution-focused techniques and empowering practice. It provides a wide range of practice examples and good reflective exercises that help illustrate how this approach works.

Milner, J and O'Byrne, P (2002) *Assessment in social work* (2nd edition). Basingstoke: Palgrave Macmillan.
A comprehensive text in terms of assessment, theories and practice frameworks set within a broader framework of social work interventions.

Parker, J (2007) The process of social work: Assessments, planning, intervention and review. In Postle, K and Lymbery, M (eds) *Social work: A companion to learning*. London: Sage.
Provides an accessible, contemporary and critical overview of the holistic art of social work assessment to aid any effective practitioner.

www.cfswp.org Centre for Social Work Practice (Tavistock Centre, London). Aims to facilitate the development of practice by promoting relationship-based approaches in social work.

www.scie.org.uk Social Care Institute for Excellence, established in 2001, to improve social care services for adults and children in the UK. Useful research publications, guidance resources which inform assessment processes.

www.brieftherapy.org.uk Brief Therapy Practice Centre, London (founded in 1989) is now Europe's largest provider of solution-focused training with over 4000 professionals from the NHS, local authorities, education and private sector attending courses each year. Their website provides useful practice notes, information regarding related publications and conferences.

www.swap.ac.uk Social Policy and Social Work Subject Centre website. Provides support for the learning and teaching communities across UK higher education. Useful downloadable resources for practitioners, students and academics.

Chapter 5
Decision-making
Graham Tooth

Introduction

Many decisions you make during your social work career will arise out of co-operation and consent among parties to a decision. However, you will regularly be faced with competing evidence and perspectives, the strength of feelings of self, service users, carers, practitioners and managers and resource limitations. In the midst of this state of flux you will seek to maintain a focus on what is relevant information for any decision. You will need to live with uncertainties about the adequacy of available evidence and best-practice decisions and manage pressure from agencies and others. You may have to swim against a tide of opinion to do what you believe is right.

Occasionally, just occasionally, you will live with a sense of doubt and limitation. Mediating within and living in this decision-making environment is the stuff of social work. Whether decision-making is co-operative or not, it is important that you develop the ability to present, reiterate and justify reasons for chosen courses of action and develop processes to help keep your bearings. This chapter explores some building blocks for effective decision-making and emphasises the importance of values in shaping those decisions.

Defining decision-making

The Oxford English Dictionary definition of decision-making includes:

> *The action of deciding (a controversy, a contest, question etc). The making up of one's mind on any point or on a course of action; a resolution or determination. The final and definite result of examining a question; a conclusion or judgement.*

ACTIVITY 5.1

- *Take a few moments and list five decisions you have made recently in your practice setting.*

- *Use these decisions to write a list or diagram of the stages you typically follow to arrive at a decision.*

- *Try this exercise as a group and see whether you come up with the same strategies for decision-making.*

Comment

Decision-making occurs all the time. It switches between small and large, minor and major, complex and simple, stressful and easy, multi-agency or single practitioner. Sometimes you will initiate a decision. At others, someone else will be asking you to act because you have access to relevant resources, skills and authority derived from legal, value or procedural requirements linked to your role. The decision may be small for you but major for the person and vice versa.

Elements of a decision-making process

So how do social workers make decisions? Figure 5.1 identifies some elements that social workers need to engage with. This diagram represents a synthesis from the research presented in this chapter and my own experience working in mental health and other settings. Although the elements appear sequentially, in everyday practice, there is an ebbing and flowing between elements.

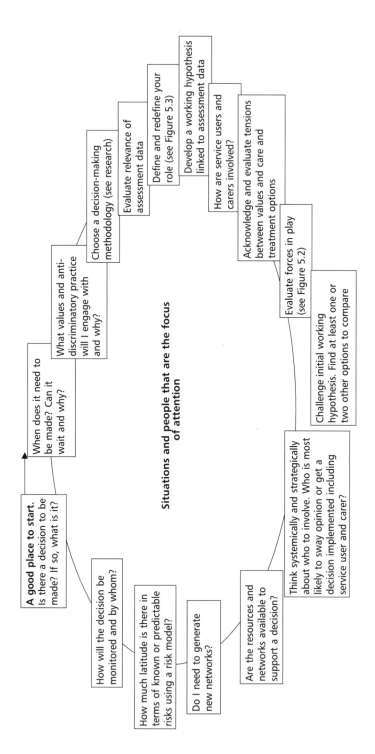

The following elements appear within the figure:

A good place to start. Is there a decision to be made? If so, what is it?

When does it need to be made? Can it wait and why?

What values and anti-discriminatory practice will I engage with and why?

Choose a decision-making methodology (see research)

Evaluate relevance of assessment data

Define and redefine your role (see Figure 5.3)

Develop a working hypothesis linked to assessment data

How are service users and carers involved?

Acknowledge and evaluate tensions between values and care and treatment options

Evaluate forces in play (see Figure 5.2)

Challenge initial working hypothesis. Find at least one or two other options to compare

Think systemically and strategically about who to involve. Who is most likely to sway opinion or get a decision implemented including service user and carer?

Are the resources and networks available to support a decision?

Do I need to generate new networks?

How much latitude is there in terms of known or predictable risks using a risk model?

How will the decision be monitored and by whom?

Situations and people that are the focus of attention

Figure 5.1 Elements of a decision-making process

Although you will be addressing these individual elements, there are two questions you need to ask yourself throughout any decision-making activity.

Firstly, which element/s in this process do I want to focus on in order to arrive at a decision? For example:

- I need to seek clarity about the hypothesis. At this point I will be contacting other networks who know the situation or reading relevant literature, for example, in relation to dementia and risk.

- Am I happy about the way the service user is being excluded from meetings? Do I need to focus on making sure the person is included?

Secondly, do I need to take charge of the process or are people managing? This last question touches on developing an ability to make effective use of your own resources of time, energy, emotional well being and assertiveness (see Chapter 9). It is also about keeping others empowered to do what they do well, whether it is a service user, carer, practitioner, manager or community group.

Is there a decision to be made?

This is such a simple question and yet there is a tendency in practice to think that because a problem is presented to us we must act. Effective assessments (see Chapter 4) will help with making this judgment but it is good practice to routinely ask:

- Is there a decision to be made here?
- If so, what is it? If not, surely there is nothing to be done.
- Is it me that needs to act?

Alternatively ask:

- Is there a problem and if so what is it?
- Does it need solving, why and why now?

Most practitioners know the experience of being part of meandering discussions about a case because these fundamental questions are not addressed. For example, the group talks about how awful or difficult the situation is with a person suffering from advanced dementia, without asking, *is there a question to be answered?* or *is there a decision to be made?*

In my own practice across the years these questions have proved invaluable in gaining clarity, creating boundaries, saving time and sometimes allowing service users and carers time to find their own solutions rather than services jumping in too quickly – empowerment. In supported care settings it is important to ask:

- What decisions do we tend to make for people?
- Is this necessary?
- How can we promote and maintain levels of independence?
- How much time do I have and what do I do in an emergency?

> **CASE STUDY**
>
> *Mary's dementia is well advanced and she cannot be left alone at home as she turns on gas and electric appliances with no awareness of safety, empties cupboards onto the floor and goes out with no sense of road awareness. She attends a day centre so her husband can have a break and attend to household issues. One day at the centre she decides she wants to go home early without support and makes to leave. Staff are aware that she does not understand basic road safety and will have trouble navigating her environment.*

Comment

There are times when you have to act quickly to ensure someone's well-being and so the thinking process will be quick and based on information you have available at the time. For Mary you will need to assess different ways to manage the situation. This will be framed around questions like: *is there anything we can do to support Mary not to leave without needing to use restraint? Could we monitor her safely in the community if she leaves?*

Mary may lack the capacity to know what she is doing. The Mental Capacity Act 2005 empowers practitioners to decide whether Mary has capacity using a two-stage test and the common-law concept of 'reasonable belief'. Reasonable belief means making a decision the best you can at the time with the knowledge and experience to hand. If your decision is later challenged, you will be able to point to objective evidence as to why Mary did or did not lack capacity. If you reasonably believe Mary lacks capacity you can then make a decision for Mary in her best interests. In Mary's case it is likely she does lack capacity to know how to keep herself safe and you would need to ensure she didn't go out alone or leave the centre at all.

After you make an emergency decision, ask yourself: *If this is likely to be an ongoing concern is this non-secure setting appropriate? Does there need to be a day centre policy and training to deal with these kinds of incidents?* Decision-making isn't just about individual practitioners – sometimes agencies need to plan ahead so practitioners know what to do when these situations arise.

Values/anti-discriminatory practice/empowering service users and carers

It can't be overstated how important values and anti-discriminatory practice are in shaping decision-making.

> **CASE STUDY**
>
> *John is currently in a deep depression (loss of motivation, a sense of no hope, thinking it would better if he was dead, believing he has failed his family). This is sapping his ability*

CASE STUDY *continued*

to make effective decisions. The team agree that John's depression is causing him to self-neglect and get into financial debt. You know that eventually he will recover his abilities and would be devastated if things are allowed to deteriorate.

ACTIVITY **5.2**

Applying different values as circumstances change

With reference to the GSCC Codes of Practice for social care (**www.gscc.org.uk**).

- What values would you use to guide decision-making in John's present situation?
- What values would you engage with as John becomes more able to make decisions again?

Comment

However little John may be able to do for himself at this time, the focus will be on supporting him to do whatever he can. This starting point means you will be supporting John's strengths, affirming his identity, encouraging him to do the little things and supporting networks and friends from the outset. At this point in John's situation, you would also be more likely to make decisions that are more directive and not give a lot of choice, as this overwhelms him. The focus would be on protecting him from harm or neglect; for example, making sure the flat gets cleaned, taking his washing to the laundrette, actively contacting financial agencies with John's consent, taking him to outpatients or arranging for mental health services to see him at home. You may get others in his network to do these things and provide support to him.

As John regains motivation and physical energy you would begin to build on promoting independence and decreasing the emphasis on a directive approach.

When does discrimination set in?

There will be a point where being directive becomes welfarist – a point where practitioners and carers assume they are experts on John's situation regardless of John recovering his abilities. Welfarism undermines John's capacity and right to make his own decisions. This point could also be marked by a disablist perspective – a point where the person with mental health problems (John) is labelled as unable to make his own decisions or is unreliable (Thompson, 1998). John becomes an object of professional curiosity and decision-making and his identity and abilities are ignored or undervalued.

I hope that you can see that the values used above are being applied relatively across time. However, some values such as respect and dignity are absolute and unchanging throughout the period of support.

Challenging stereotypes and decision-making

Often you will experience joint practice that is in tune with current values. However, there will be times when you will need to adopt an active role and challenge contemporary discriminations and promote a more democratic and humane way of living. You will need to decide how power relations are to be shaped, challenged and managed.

Dominelli (2002) outlines three types of power used in relation to disadvantaged groups.

- **Power over** Practitioners and society make decisions for groups even if this is not justified. This is characterised by dominance over others and favours the dominant group. For example, services assuming that older people should be in risk-free environments (care home) rather than live at home.

- **Power to** People and groups exercise agency to resist oppressive situations. Older people are able to speak out, perhaps with the help of others including social workers to claim the right to take risks.

- **Power of** People and groups draw on collective strengths to achieve a common goal. Through national organisations for older people and the famous older generation a movement is developing that challenges current stereotypes of older people and demands different services. You could consider drawing on the strength of such movements by helping service users engage with them.

Finally, it is worth considering how much change the service user or carer wants. In many situations people have little choice but to go through the experience of big changes in life but it is worth asking what the person thinks is momentous and what is small. De Mello (1997) cites this story. A man had lived in his house for 50 years and suddenly moved next door. Surprised local reporters asked why. The man replied '*I guess it's the gypsy in me.*' A small change but a huge adventure.

Evaluating assessment information

The content of assessment tools and proformas is shaped by agency policy and purpose, laws, practitioners, research (service user, carer and practitioner) and values. Implicitly or explicitly all assessment formats guide the practitioner to a conclusion about the relevance of the contents in each tool. For example, assessment focused on a social model (role changes, housing insecurity, wandering at night, debt, harassment, etc.) may omit relevant biological or psychological needs. Similarly, a psychiatric diagnosis for dementia is likely to focus on biological and cognitive processes rather than the service user's worry about his/her partner's failing physical health, financial stress or elder abuse as factors causing confusion or anxiety.

No one assessment tool is better or worse than another. The choice to be made is which tools are likely to provide the most useful assessment to help with decision-making that reflects the service user's or carer's circumstances. Time and risks permitting, a legitimate decision may be to seek further assessment.

CASE STUDY

Domestic violence and depression

Jean is 75 years old and presented to services with symptoms of depression. Jean's husband was upset at her withdrawal from household tasks and wanted help as this was disrupting the division of labour at home and causing arguments. Jean's withdrawal was interpreted by practitioners as a sign of depression and Jean was prescribed medication. At subsequent home visits by a mental health worker to support activities and recovery, Jean revealed a long and continuing history of domestic violence that had not be asked about at assessment. Lawrence (2008) highlights how domestic violence is routinely under-investigated for older people.

CASE STUDY

A difficult person who can't be helped or someone struggling with meaning and purpose?

Sixty-year-old Malcolm had a stroke that caused significant right-sided paralysis and mental confusion. Prior to his stroke he was an active community member. He was refusing necessary home care and practitioners expressed frustration and considered withdrawing services which would have precipitated a crisis. Luckily, a worker took the time to ask him about what his beliefs told him about dealing with adversity and receiving help. Malcolm replied, accept your fate, medication should be avoided, stand on your own two feet, it is important to be able to give. Subsequently, someone with a similar faith was found to talk this through and Malcolm accepted help.

Assessment tools are an essential part of any practitioner's repertoire. However, any tool may leave out important information or the assessor may omit to ask important questions. As a decision-maker you need to satisfy yourself that relevant information has been gathered as part of the decision-making process. Ask yourself and others:

- What assessment tools have been used?

- Does their content represent a holistic picture of the service user's or carer's situation?

- Have relevant questions been asked and adequately answered?

- Are the assessment tools up to date and effectively used?

Until recently, domestic violence and gender, race and sexuality discrimination were absent from assessment forms. Spirituality and religion are on most forms but practitioners rarely explore or record these critical areas of some people's lives. Good supervision, researching and connecting with anti-discriminatory practice will keep this area alive for you.

Generating a working hypothesis – unless you know why there is a problem you can't know how to address it

Are the symptoms of depression or anxiety arising because of poverty, discrimination, poor housing, spiritual conflict or doubt, isolation, family relationships, grief, biological dysfunction, role change conflict, a network problem, lack of service creativity? Can s/he help acting in this way or is s/he responsible for her behaviour? How big is the risk? Is it a combination of factors and which ones are most important to target to achieve change? These debates ring daily round the country as practitioners grapple with how to find solutions to diverse lifestyles and circumstances.

Mental health teams regularly debate whether aggressive behaviour could be viewed as an aspect of mental illness, a feature of personality or culture, a reflection of childhood family abuse, an indication of social isolation linked to paranoia, poverty leading to financial stress, persecution by local youths or the poor response of agencies (mental health teams, housing or social security) to requests for help or support in times of need.

Service user and carer research (Faulkner and Layzell, 2000) emphasises the importance of asking the person what helps or what might make a difference, even where you might be invoking statutory or duty of care actions.

For each 'why is this happening' hypothesis above, there will be 'how to resolve it' interventions. Below are five actions to help with hypothesising.

- Gather relevant research, theory and values that help to hypothesise about the 'why' of a problem.

- Get to know what the service user, carers, networks, communities and practitioners think about why there is a problem and what to do about it.

- Settle on a working hypothesis for why the problem exists, even if this is tentative. It may be the best you can get at the time.

- Develop a 'how to resolve it' working hypothesis.

- Check that there is a link between the 'why' and the 'how to resolve it' hypotheses.

Without some clarity in this process you will not be able to evaluate outcomes, engage others meaningfully or justify your interventions.

CASE STUDY

You are the social worker assessing a situation in which Eric has come to an office appointment concerned about having to physically restrain his wife Alice, who has dementia. When you meet he says he is fatigued by being kept awake part of most nights and trying to stop Alice leaving the house, as she is considered to be unsafe and would get lost. He restrains her and this is causing bruising on her arms and cuts where she knocks against furniture in the struggles. He can't think of another way of dealing with the situation and now seems desperate for some kind of help.

Your initial 'why' hypothesis might be that Eric is a well-intentioned husband who needs to know his wife is safe. He can cope with being awake at night but not with her persistent attempts to leave the house. The 'how to resolve it' hypothesis might lead to the use of sedation (medical solution), telecare support, night-sitters or respite (social solutions). Day care or counselling and support around role changes are unlikely to link to solving the problem.

Eric is reluctant but agrees to you visiting Alice at home. When you arrive the house looks clean and well cared for. However, when you see Alice she looks malnourished and her clothing smells strongly of urine. Eric won't allow her to answer your questions and prevents Alice from moving from the armchair. Eventually Eric insists you leave, saying there is no problem and he doesn't know why he asked you for help in the first place.

Your 'why' hypothesis will now have shifted with the evidence to the likelihood that Eric is abusing Alice and that his intentions are not in Alice's best interests. The original 'how to resolve it' hypothesis will have shifted away from supporting Eric's benign concerns to one of protecting Alice. The 'how to resolve it' question will not now be about a small piece of additional care and will shift to considering what needs to be done to protect Alice from abuse.

Risk and decision-making

Risk is currently the subject of much debate in society and looms large in most decision-making discussions. For each person you help, it is necessary to have a grasp of which risk models are being used.

Morgan (2000) describes a model of positive risk-taking within mental health services based on:

- developing plans that reflect the stated priorities of the service user;
- weighing up the potential benefits and harms of exercising one choice of action over another;
- identifying and using positive potentials in the person, her/his environment, carers or services;
- using available resources and support to achieve desired outcomes and to minimise potential harmful outcomes.

Along with other risk-taking models, Morgan's acts as an antidote to potential and sometimes unintended policy and practice pressures towards risk elimination rather than minimisation. For example, reducing suicides among people with mental disorder (DoH, 1999c) or reducing falls among older people (DoH, 2001a).

CASE STUDY

Harry has an acquired brain injury following a road accident. He lives with his wife Louise and their three children. Harry returned home a year ago from a period of rehabilitation. Louise reports to social services that she is physically and emotionally at the end of the line unless something changes. By degrees Harry is verbally disinhibited in public and at home, he is unable to concentrate to help with daily family tasks, he has little idea of the value of money or the need to pay bills and takes money from Louise's purse without asking. Harry says he is happy being at home and says he can change.

Comment

A positive risk-taking model seeks to build on the strengths in Harry's way of being and social networks. A positive risk-taking model suggests more needs to be found out about Harry than just the problems above. Harry sees his future at home and Louise has not entirely shut the door yet. The benefits for Harry of a home and family life could be huge. Similarly the opportunity, with help, to manage his verbal lack of inhibition or for practitioners and others to engage the local community in an understanding of brain injury could relieve tensions arising because of stigma. Louise and the children might gain a great sense of achievement and belonging to know they have kept Harry at home.

Positive risk-taking is a good starting point for any decision-making. However, in Harry's case it also needs to be balanced out with a realistic evaluation of risks to family breakdown, long-term mental health issues for children and Louise, and financial insolvency. From a value base perspective there are tensions between Louise's right to stop caring and choose another life course and the need for Harry to have lifelong support and any emotional benefits that might accrue. A positive risk-taking focus can overemphasise Harry's needs above other important dilemmas and risks. Different risk models need to be used alongside each other.

Other forces shaping decision-making

The knowledge and value bases acquired by practitioners to assess and intervene are important to effective decision-making. There is a constantly developing state of knowledge about social, spiritual, biological and psychological factors affecting people's lives. Such understandings have developed more humane responses to behaviours that were previously not understood; for example, autism, challenging behaviours, brain injury and dementia.

However, Figure 5.2 shows other potent forces at work in shaping decision-making. As a general rule of thumb these forces will be time-, location- and agency-specific and demand of the social worker that s/he maintains an up-to-date awareness.

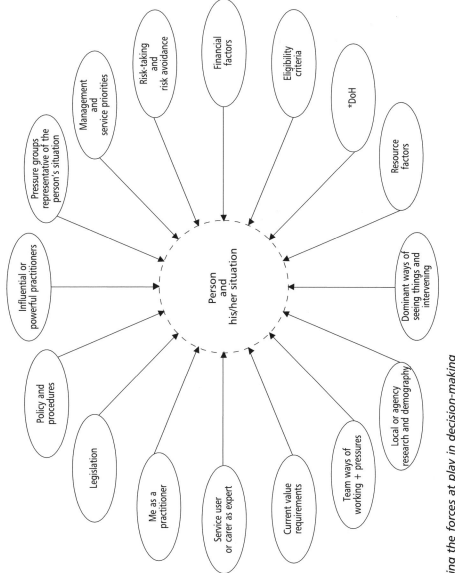

Figure 5.2 Analysing the forces at play in decision-making
*Department of Health

Political forces include media or government attitudes to risk; individual rights and duties versus community responsibility and capacity (how far should family and community carry the burden of caring or will the state provide?); the promotion of domestic violence and adult abuse as no longer acceptable. Citizen-led forces include service users and carers as experts in their own lives, campaigning to stop domestic violence, campaigns for the rights of gay people. Economic forces include the money and resources available to develop and provide services. Value forces include challenges to racism, sexism, classism in accessing education and numerous other current discriminations. Dominant ways of seeing could include the use of 'power over' (Dominelli, 2002) medical perspectives in assessment and intervention.

ACTIVITY **5.3**

Choose a service user or carer situation you are involved with. Use Figure 5.2 to consider the following questions.

- *Which forces would you want to raise or reduce the profiles of?*

- *Which forces are beyond your control?*

- *Which resources or people might you engage to manage these forces?*

Comment

Figure 5.2 demonstrates the number of variables that might be in play for any decision. This variety can be a source of great possibility in so far as any elements put together have great power to act positively. They are also important as you can draw on authority from a range of sources to justify a decision. For example, combining policy, values on service user involvement, pressure group influence, laws on discrimination and statutory funding to ensure a person can access care services and make her/his own risk decisions.

Here are some ideas about how other forces influence decision-making. The outcome of local service user and carer consultations may affect how care is given for minority ethnic groups. National reactions to the latest local or national tragic event (suicide, murder) may lead to risk avoidance that challenges the service value of promoting independence. Neglect in a care home may lead to social work reviews directed towards monitoring restricted areas of concern rather than quality of life care planning.

In this environment you may develop an idea of what a preferred decision might look like but be unable to implement it. It is important to remember that a decision is not a decision unless it can be implemented.

Policies change but decision-making thrives

The current policy trend for adults is towards self-directed support (DoH, 2007a, b) based on self-assessment by a person whereby needs are represented by outcomes.

Money is then allocated to her/him to reach those outcomes. This represents a shift in decision-making away from practitioners to service users and to managers implementing financial formulae to apportion money. However, social workers will continue to support people through the self-directed process, to make complex decisions in relation to the most vulnerable and to support those unable to make their own decisions. Decision-making will continue to thrive.

Policy promotion and society today tend to use the language of superlatives that set up expectations of the 'most' radical and creative thinking, the 'best' innovative change, 'full' assessments and 'inclusive' partnerships that will 'transform' well-being and lead to 'fulfilled' lives. The public are told practitioners will deliver. As a practitioner it is difficult not to be affected by this pressure. While many recent policy changes are to be applauded, there is a need to acknowledge with a degree of humility that many service users want to maintain an ordinary quality of life and that services and practitioners do not always have the knowledge or resources to bring about tumultuous changes (Munro, 2003; Brandon, 2000). Try to keep a mental note of how you are responding and staying creative in the culture of perfection.

Partnership and networking

Partnerships, networks and multi-agency working are crucial to effective decision-making. Chapter 3 covers this in detail and it is useful to refer back to the comments sections there to see how you might respond to the questions below.

ACTIVITY 5.4

Take time now to reflect on the quality of decision-making partnerships in your work setting.

- *Are they supportive and consistent and do they help you to analyse and understand?*
- *Do they assist with resources and flexible responses to diverse situations?*
- *Are you doing all you can to support and develop partnerships? There is a tendency for practitioners to focus only on what others can do and to neglect this question.*

Paying attention to yourself

The daily expectations and pressures on social workers to make best decisions will inevitably raise tensions and conflicts, especially where services are unable to provide for a service user's needs or outcome-based services. You may feel ill equipped to find a way forward; situations are complex and volatile and decisions are finely judged. This is a reality of working life and everyone goes there at some time or another. You may also have unreasonably high expectations of yourself. Figure 5.3 outlines some personal anchors that can be useful when making decisions.

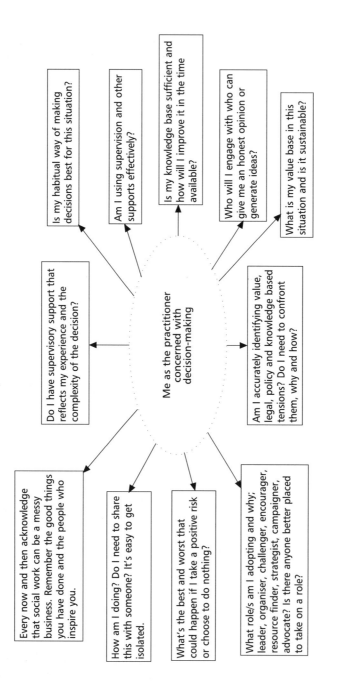

Figure 5.3 Paying attention to myself

ACTIVITY **5.5**

Spend some time reflecting on these questions.

- *Find a metaphor, other than 'anchor', that works for you.*

- *How do you approach decision-making? For example, do you jump in with both feet and get people organised? Do you just want to get things sorted to relieve your own or others' worries? Do you tend to sit back and let things happen? Do you find making decisions difficult? Do you have a patient and measured approach?*

Comment

There is nothing inherently right or wrong in different ways of decision-making. Each approach has to be judged on its value as part of the decision-making process. However, you do need to be able to recognise your preferred styles so you can adjust.

And lastly, be clear what you want from others. They will find it a lot easier to give something if they know what you want, whether it is a request for emotional support, expert advice, clarification or action. These issues are explored further in Chapters 9,10 and 11.

RESEARCH SUMMARY

Munro (2003) reviews two types of decision-making. The first is pattern recognition, which is often used by experienced and knowledgeable workers engaging intuition (practice experience), sifting information selectively, metaphor and storytelling. Pattern recognition biases decision-making towards 'satisficing'. This means the tendency to settle on the first good-enough solution that presents itself even if it is not the best available.

Pattern recognition can work well for less significant or less complex decisions. For example, relieving poverty through a benefits application, treating biological depression pharmacologically or arranging home care. Practitioners can rapidly develop a story around a person's situation based on practice experience of similar situations and some process of checking with the person or others. Experienced practitioners run the risk of excluding important information when using pattern recognition. Inexperienced practitioners run a similar risk but due to lack of knowledge of what information is important for any presenting problem.

In contrast to pattern recognition, formal decision-making follows a prescribed set of questions, a process that aims to think broadly and to generate several options for intervention. The processes and information are represented through a decision-making-tree tool. Advantages might include having a wide range of information available about the person and her/his circumstances, generation of a wide range of options for intervention, transparency and a best-outcomes decision. The main disadvantages are that it can be time-consuming, unnecessary information is collected, service users' and carers' privacy is unnecessarily intruded on and resources may not be available.

RESEARCH SUMMARY *continued*

Gambrill (2006) discusses research on how decisions are made, outlines useful bullet-pointed lists and charts and describes barriers to effective decision-making. Gambrill's research overview on decision-making highlights that:

- *similar decision-making processes are common to all areas of human activity;*
- *you can improve the quality of your decision-making capacity;*
- *reflection and thinking time are crucial to effective consideration of factors relevant to the decision at hand;*
- *barriers that prevent effective decision-making need to be identified, interpreted and removed wherever possible;*
- *it is important to have contact with others who will encourage lateral and focused thinking and if necessary challenge you;*
- *mistakes will happen but you can learn from them.*

Edmund (2008) has developed an 11-stage process based on an analysis of decision-making across a wide range of occupational groups. His Shortened Standard Model 4 (SM4) format contains the four elements:

- *problem definition;*
- *alternatives sought by searching for information and generating solutions;*
- *evaluating or selecting the best option based on evidence;*
- *challenging or checking whether this is the best option.*

Edmund also urges you to work creatively, to engage with your own resourcefulness.

The thousands of effective and creative decisions that practitioners make daily rarely come to public light. Occasionally things can and do go wrong. The essence of effective practice, whether things go right or wrong, is captured by Munro (2003) when she says that decisions should not be judged by their outcome: fallibility is an inevitable aspect of the work. They should be judged on the way they were reached. *Popper, cited in Gambrill (2006, p198) emphasises a practitioner's need to* recognise our duty to minimize avoidable mistakes.

ACTIVITY **5.6**

- *Briefly review one decision you made recently. Which of the methods above did you use and why?*
- *What messages do Munro's and Popper's comments above carry for you?*
- *What actions will you take now to develop your decision-making abilities?*

C H A P T E R   S U M M A R Y

This chapter has explored ways of structuring thinking and actions for effective decision-making. It has reviewed the influence of values, anti-discriminatory practices and the wider forces that shape decision-making. It makes the case that social work holds an almost unique role among other helping groups in needing to take a holistic view of situations when making decisions and in being concerned with how social forces and the distribution of power affect outcomes. As such you will need to develop and maintain a familiarity with the wide range of variables addressed in this chapter as they apply to your service setting. The points below give some ideas for staying alive to decision-making as a skill in its own right.

- Develop your ability to describe the process you travelled to arrive at a decision and include your ability to challenge your own hypotheses.

- Actively cultivate your internal and external supports and reflective capabilities using the ideas in this chapter. Ask yourself, *what can I do to develop a healthy resilience so that the pressures of decision-making don't leave me overwhelmed or detached?*

- Clarify the values and value tensions inherent in any decision-making activity and be prepared to swim against the tide of opinion to support what you believe to be right.

FURTHER READING

DoH (2007) *Independence, choice and risk: A guide to best practice in supported decision-making.* London: The Stationery Office.
Includes a supported decision tool focused on risk.

Segal, J, et al. (2007) *Depression in older adults and the elderly.* **www.helpguide.org/mental/depression/elderly.htm**
Provides a summary of signs and causes of depression and suggests kinds of decisions.

Knott, C and Scragg, T (2007) *Reflective practice in social work.* Exeter: Learning Matters.
A good introduction to the reflective process essential for effective decision-making.

O'Sullivan, T (1999) *Decision-making in social work.* Basingstoke: Macmillan.
Very helpful and succinct information and discussions that develop the knowledge and practice issues contained in this chapter.

Taylor, B and Devine, T (1995) *Assessing needs and planning care in social work.* Aldershot: Ashgate.
Includes a section on decision-making and some useful diagrams and charts.

Milner, J and O'Byrne, P (1998) *Assessment in social work.* Basingstoke: Macmillan.
Contains a section on prospect theory (barriers to effective decision-making and risk).

Chapter 6

Skills for collaborative working
Teri Cranmer and Janet McCray

This chapter will help you to meet the following National Occupational Standards:

Key Role 2: Plan, carry out, review and evaluate social work practice, with individuals, families, carers, groups, communities and other professionals.

- Develop and maintain relationships with individuals, families, carers, groups, communities and others.
- Work with individuals, families, carers, groups, communities and others to avoid crisis situations and address problems and conflict.
- Examine with individuals, families, carers, groups, communities and others support networks which can be accessed and developed.
- Work with individuals, families, carers, groups, communities and others to initiate and sustain support networks.
- Contribute to the development and evaluation of support networks.
- Help groups to achieve planned outcomes for their members and to evaluate the appropriateness of their work.

This chapter will also you achieve the following key social work benchmarks (Quality Assurance Agency for Higher Education, 2008):

- Work in partnership with service users and carers and other professionals to foster dignity, choice and independence, and effect change.
- The relationship between agency policies, legal requirements and professional boundaries in shaping the nature of services provided in interdisciplinary contexts and the issues associated with working across professional boundaries and within different disciplinary groups.
- The factors and processes that facilitate effective interdisciplinary, interprofessional and interagency collaboration and partnership.
- Involve users of social work services in ways that increase their resources, capacity and power to influence factors affecting their lives.
- Consult actively with others, including service users and carers, who hold relevant information or expertise.
- Act cooperatively with others, liaising and negotiating across differences such as organisational and professional boundaries and differences of identity or language.
- Develop effective helping relationships and partnerships with other individuals, groups and organisations that facilitate change.

Introduction

The International Association of Schools of Social Work and the International Federation of Social Workers (2001) describe social work as a profession which:

> *Promotes social change, problem solving in human relationships and the empowerment and liberation of people to enhance well-being.*

> (Skills for Care, 2008)

This cannot be achieved in isolation, and as the QAA notes:

> *Social work takes place in an inter-agency context, and social workers work collaboratively with others towards interdisciplinary and cross-professional objectives.*

> (QAA, 2008, p5)

At the centre of all practice is the person who requires support.

Bringing values, goals, differing agendas and needs to create change through collaboration is an exciting and challenging prospect. Yet it can also seem daunting and complicated. In this chapter strategies for making collaboration effective will be presented. The starting point will be a review of definitions and their meaning. Collaboration as a practice will be explored, while other language and terms often used interchangeably will be clarified. Components of good collaborative practice and strategies for its development are outlined. Key policy and legislation, general protocols and practice will be charted. Examples of good practice with adults underpin the chapter content as some barriers to collaboration are considered. During the chapter attention is paid to frameworks to aid fair and appropriate social work practice.

What is collaborative working?

A useful starting point is Quinney (2006, p11), who offers a lexicon of terms used in social work practice. Her book, *Collaborative practice in social work* (2006) in the Learning Matters series, explores the subject in depth. A simple definition of collaborative working is:

> *A respect for other professionals and service users and their skills and from this starting point, an agreed sharing of authority, responsibility and resources aimed at specific outcomes or actions, and gained through cooperation and consensus.*

> (McCray, 2007a, p132)

Often collaborative working forms an element of multi-professional and multi-agency teamwork (Taylor, 2006, p19) while other terms such as multi-professional and multi-disciplinary are also used to mean the same thing.

These definitions provide information on what the intention and goals of collaborative working are, but the process of collaboration can take a number of forms.

> ### RESEARCH SUMMARY
>
> *Findings on forms of collaborative working*
>
> *Davey, et al. (2004, p134) draw attention to the formal and informal models of colla-borative working in social work with older people. They suggest that informal arrange-ments based on practitioner-driven activity are as influential for people using services as formal arrangements such as those in integrated care teams where health and social care agencies work within a formal strategically agreed framework to deliver a particular service. The writers continue their research to look at collaboration with general practi-tioners (GPs) in older people's services (Davey et al., 2005, p399). One finding is that informal collaborative practice, which moved away from organisational or formal frame-works, was needed to work through some of the very real differences that different professionals held and the challenges of tight resources (Davey et al., 2004, p134). What was important was the informal relationships built with other professionals, perhaps through other networking activity, educational events or other contact.*

Comment

Research shows that no one form of collaborative working can succeed on its own. While successive governments have created legislation and formal frameworks for collaboration, often it is grass roots workers who can make things happen based on their informal networks and connections to others, created through a shared commit-ment to service users. As Andy Mantell sets out in Chapter 1, often it is the building of relationships which makes or breaks good practice arrangements with other profes-sionals and service users. However, other factors also play their part and will become of more significance if the social work role and intervention is complex.

Components of good practice

Many of the elements of good practice in collaboration such as communication, team working and knowledge of the roles of other professionals and workers have been described as 'common sense' by some professional undergraduate students (Gordon and Marshall, 2007, p47). Valuing other professional roles and contributions may also seem obvious. Of course no one would dispute these knowledge and skills and their importance as central in developing collaborative practice. What also needs to be considered are their components. Increasingly, older people in receipt of services are partners in their assessment and support processes, while other agency partners may also be involved.

As we talk about communication, what do we mean? What form might it take and how important is the context in which the communication takes place? For example, positive communication may be easy in routine information-sharing activity by email or at an informal meeting with another professional. As you will know, some situations in practice are much more challenging for everyone involved. Begley and Monaghan (2004, p22) write of the ethical dilemmas faced by professionals when disclosing a dementia diagnosis to individuals. They note the importance of collaboration with the service user and the critical role of inter-professional communication. What is important is clear, consistent information and responses from all involved, yet the different values held by professionals may mean communication is difficult. For example, not all professionals involved might want to give full information to the person in receipt of the diagnosis. It may not be appropriate as they might not be qualified to give a full answer. Mixed messages can be given to an individual which ultimately impact on future communication, support to the person and collaborative working.

Talking about values may also seem a 'given' in collaboration. McCray (2007b, p254) observes that personal values are something that individuals hold at the centre of their being. Values are developed over time and from experience, and personal values may reflect an individual's culture, moral stance or lifestyle.

When it comes to professional values another layer of strongly held and learnt beliefs is added. All may be fine until there is a clash of professional values, for example when ethics are at issue as in the above case and a decision on action needs to be taken. One group of professionals might see themselves as the rightful lead and final decision-holder in a case, based on the perceived value of their profession and its status. Hugman (1991) has written about inter-professional competition (Borthwick et al., 2008) and the struggle to hold virtuoso or high-status roles by some groups of professionals. In collaborative practice a desire to hold higher status might get in the way of listening to the person needing support and their views and expectations about what they need.

Exploring the research on components of good practice shows that at times the givens of good collaboration might not be as easy to address as at first glance. Working with people who have complicated lives and lifestyles can impact on the degree and quality of communication in collaboration that takes place. As professionals are faced with ethical challenges and conflict around values, it is important that you are prepared to face up to, or prevent, any potential problems at an early stage. An important point here is not to make assumptions about the seemingly straightforward aspects of good collaboration.

CASE STUDY

Doreen and her Alzheimer's disease diagnosis
You are working with Doreen and a team of professionals from health and social care. Doreen has recently been diagnosed with Alzheimer's disease. Doreen lives with her partner Jack in a small city-centre flat. Their only son Anthony was killed in a car accident three years ago. At a meeting with the consultant and other healthcare professionals it was suggested that it may be better not to give Doreen the full extent of her diagnosis as it was felt it might compound the feelings of depression and helplessness she had described since her son's death. As the social worker you do not agree with this view and feel the collaboration across professional groups was likely to be less successful and impact on communication with Doreen and Jack. You seek to understand why other professionals felt this was the correct intervention.

ACTIVITY **6.1**

Consider your thoughts and feelings about Doreen's situation.

Write down what you think has created a difference of opinion with other professionals on information given to Doreen.

What are the positive and negative consequences of going along with the consultant's view from a collaborative perspective?

What action would you need to take to ensure all professionals supported your position?

Comment

You will know from your earlier reading that often professional viewpoints on ethical decision-making are related to their initial professional education. Your professional position is founded on a belief in empowering social work relationships so that clients can influence person-centred decision-making (Gates, 2006). Doctors and other professionals also have their own professional values. Knowing about these and their basis is helpful in understanding and not judging other professionals. It is also important to avoid stereotyping other professionals and service users by making assumptions about their commonly held qualities.

To get past barriers to collaboration and gain good communication and consistent honest messages for Doreen and Jack, you will need to work on your own self-awareness and any stereotypes you may hold. Plan, direct and review your collaborative activity and intervention from a user-centred position at all times. Use straightforward language and avoid jargon. Work to influence professionals to start from this shared common purpose which strengthens rather than diminishes relationships and communication.

Collaboration for positive outcomes

You have learnt about the importance for collaboration of understanding components of other professional roles and their foundation. The context that is the social, economic and historical landscape in which professionals practise is also significant (McCray, 2003). Adult services have undergone vast change in the last decades as the move from institutional to individualised care has taken place. Understandably this has impacted on how some professionals are viewed, valued and organised. For newly qualified professionals such change should not result in role conflict, but for more established professionals, policy directives may create dissonance. This is a type of stress caused by an expectation to act in a way that is contradictory to the role they prepared for. It might manifest itself as hostility or negativity, a seeming lack of commitment and conflict in collaborative working. Understanding the context and its possible impact on the collaborative activity in process can help you decide on a strategy to ensure positive outcomes for the person in receipt of services.

The availability of resources and who should or can authorise their use or scope will also be a key issue in collaborative working. Only through agreement on the use of resources can collaboration work with trust and openness. Lingard et al. (2004) refer to 'trade' between professionals in collaborative working and its potential impact on present and future working relationships. Lingard et al. (2004) refer to this as trade in concrete commodities such as physical equipment and funding as well as social commodities such as goodwill and knowledge. In their study the authors noted the challenges of identifying the often intricate rules around trade in resources and the tension this created. For positive collaborative working transparency was vital. The authors also viewed understanding the tensions and conflict around resources as paramount to maintaining balance in a teamwork setting.

Social workers in adult services need to have a good knowledge and understanding of the context in which the collaborative activity is taking place. Changes occurring in service delivery may impact on professional interaction and the capacity and stamina of professional partners for collaboration. Clarity around funding can lessen tension and reduce conflict for collaborative partners. As a social work professional you should:

- keep up to date on social and health care policy for older people;

- regularly contact and meet with colleagues from other professional groups and exchange information on change and its impact;

- take up opportunities for shared multi-professional education whenever possible;

- when resources are an issue, recognise the need for openness and provide updates on funding or knowledge as promised.

All of these actions can help you understand and work with other professionals effectively and enable you to be clear about boundaries for different professional intervention. Credibility and trust are gained through feedback and/or delivery on resources by an agreed time.

Transforming social care through effective collaboration

Working collaboratively with people and agencies is a key factor in all new government legislation, policy and guidance. In April 2009 the Audit Commission introduced Comprehensive Area Assessment, a new assessment framework that will measure performance across local public bodies, providing a snapshot of the effectiveness of local partnerships to deliver local priorities.

Within the health and social care arena joint working and collaboration are fundamental to the modernisation agenda. The Department of Health publication *Modernising social services* (1998) set out a framework for improving joint working between health and social services, for example through the introduction of pooled budgets. A review of the changes implemented since then, *Modernising adult social care – what's working* (DoH, 2007b), highlights the tensions and successes of working in a more collaborative framework.

The modernisation agenda has emphasised the need for collaboration across agencies to enable effective partnership working. The personalisation agenda leads us into effective collaboration with people who use services and their carers. *Putting people first: A shared vision and commitment to the transformation of adult social care* (DoH, 2007a) and the local authority circular *Transforming social care* (DoH, 2008b) makes it clear that authentic partnership working is integral to a truly personalised care system. Personalisation cannot be achieved without collaboration across local authorities, the NHS, other statutory agencies, third- and private-sector providers, users and carers and the wider local community, and taking into account housing, benefits, leisure, transport and health needs.

An example of good collaborative working

A recent government initiative to promote and drive forward good collaborative working is the Department of Health POPP (Partnerships for Older People Projects) pilot project. POPPs have been set up to test person-centred and joined-up approaches from health, social care, Department of Work and Pensions and voluntary-sector agencies, in order to promote health, well-being and independence for older people, prevent unplanned admissions to hospital and delay admissions to residential care.

Adults' services in West Sussex have used POPPs funding to develop community partnership teams (CPTs). The aim of the CPTs is to support older people to stay healthy and remain independent, preventing or at least delaying the need to access long-term mainstream statutory services. The teams consist of health advisers (nurses), social workers, advisers from the Pension Service, trained support workers from local voluntary organisations and volunteers. What makes the CPTs different is that they are multi-disciplinary and multi-agency teams providing low-level provision focusing on prevention for those who don't meet statutory service-eligibility criteria. There is a single point of contact with open access, a holistic approach and continuity of worker from assessment through to follow-up.

CASE STUDY

Enabling Eileen to live a more fulfilling life
Eileen is 90 years of age and lives alone. A recent fall resulted in a fractured pelvis and five weeks in hospital. Eileen is now housebound due to her reduced mobility and lack of confidence, and she is lonely and isolated. She has agreed to a referral to the CPT. Within 48 hours a worker from the team has visited Eileen and together they have decided on the goals and actions that will enable her to live a more fulfilling life.

Goals
- *Conquer fear of falling and eventually get out again.*
- *Access practical assistance.*
- *Access benefits advice.*
- *Reduce effects of loneliness.*

Actions

- Appropriate walking aids arranged.
- Referred to falls clinic with ongoing health trainer support.
- Practical services arranged.
- Referred to Department for Work and Pensions re Attendance Allowance.
- WRVS Cars and Companions arranged.

This intervention has had positive outcomes for Eileen: she now feels safer and significantly less at risk of falls, the additional services have led to improved self-esteem and ability to live independently, her income has increased as she now receives Attendance Allowance and she is feeling less isolated.
(Potter, 2008, personal communication)

Comment

For a team such as the CPT to be effective there has to be a cohesiveness that goes beyond having a multi-agency, multi-disciplinary 'one-stop shop' approach. Integral to cohesion is sharing: sharing values, knowledge, skills, records and information. As previously discussed in this chapter, team members need to develop trust in one another and accept that all roles are of equal value and importance; sharing values, knowledge and skills helps to build this level of team spirit. However, sharing records and information can create an ethical dilemma. There is a legal responsibility under the Data Protection Act 1998 to keep personal information secure and confidential; it should only be shared with other organisations and individuals with the consent of the person (see Chapter 8).

ACTIVITY 6.2

By definition a multi-agency team consists of other organisations. Does this mean that information cannot be shared with other team members? Write down what you think the boundaries to sharing information are. What checks and balances need to be in place to ensure that personal information is respected?

Comment

Some staff may feel more at ease sharing information between statutory organisations but be more reticent about being open with workers from other sectors or with volunteers. There is no rationale for this – a team cannot collaborate effectively if important information is kept secret or only partially shared. Goble (2008, p132) tells us that a collaborative culture requires a commitment to ensure that the correct information is shared at the right time and in the right format among the people who need to know that the best outcomes can be achieved for the service user.

You need to ask permission to share personal information and explain what you will share with whom and the purpose of sharing it. It is good practice to ask a person to give you a signed permission to share their information and to state on this who they agree or disagree to having information about them. If someone lacks the capacity to consent to the sharing of their information, section 5 of the Mental Capacity Act 2005 (DoH, 2005) allows this as long as it is in the best interests of the person. On occasions you may find yourself with a legal obligation to share information without the person's consent (for example, if a vulnerable person was at risk of harm) but in these circumstances you would generally inform the person that you were going to take this action.

Fletcher gives us six questions to consider each time we are intending to share information or break confidentiality.

- What benefit will flow from this development?

- What invasion of personal liberty does it entail?

- Is it possible to achieve the benefit without the invasion?

- How do we inform and involve service users?

- Is confidential information compromised?

- Are the consequences of not sharing information greater than those of doing so?

(Fletcher, 2006, p54)

Shared recording can create similar ethical dilemmas within a multi-agency team; agreement to share information is a prerequisite of shared record-keeping as anything recorded will be accessed by other workers in the team. Joint files can also raise personal issues for some staff. It is one thing for your manager to access your case files but quite another for your peers to be looking over your shoulder. Some workers may feel uncomfortable or threatened by this level of openness and accountability within a team, particularly if they feel that other team members are more experienced or qualified than they are. In Chapter 8 Gill Constable explores record-keeping in more detail to increase your understanding.

C H A P T E R   S U M M A R Y

This chapter has explored the exciting possibilities and challenges of collaboration. You have read of the need to work informally as well as formally with other professionals to get good results. It is important to recognise different professional perspectives on giving information to service users. Values may be different across professional groups and they can impact on communication and positions about ethics and confidentiality. Tight resources may play a part in a reluctance to collaborate from some professionals, while different views on confidentiality and sharing of information could hinder effective collaborative practice. In your reading of this chapter you will have found that for the social worker prepared and equipped to move beyond the perceived givens and assumptions about multi-agency working, and other professional roles, there are many learning opportunities. Positive collaborative working offers the chance to look critically at your own practice within a team setting and offers the tools to create new strategies for co-operation in challenging ethical situations. At all times there is potential to learn from and value the positions and contributions of other professionals and people who use services and their families, who through the vehicle of collaborative working are enabled to retain control.

Barton, C (2007) Allies and enemies: The service user as care coordinator. In Weinstein, J, Whittington, C and Leiba, T (eds) *Collaboration in social work practice.* London: Jessica Kingsley. This chapter tells it how it is for real people, real situations. It concludes with good-practice guidelines to enable effective collaboration.

Davis, J and Sims, D (2007) Shared values in interprofessional collaboration. In Weinstein, J, Whittington, C and Leiba, T (eds) *Collaboration in social work practice.* London: Jessica Kingsley. This chapter considers where and how social work values overlap with those of the health professions.

Chapter 7

Negotiation skills in practice: Implications for practitioners and service users
Chris Smethurst and Rebecca Long

A C H I E V I N G A S O C I A L W O R K D E G R E E

This chapter will help you to meet the following National Occupational Standards:

Key Role 1: Prepare for, and work with individuals, families, carers, groups and communities to assess their needs and circumstances.

- Work with individuals, families, carers, groups and communities to enable them to analyse, identify, clarify and express their strengths, expectations and limitations.
- Work with individuals, families, carers, groups and communities to enable them to assess and make informed decisions about their needs, circumstances, risks, preferred options and resources.

Key Role 2: Plan, carry out, review and evaluate social work practice, with individuals, families, carers, groups, communities and other professionals.

- Develop and maintain relationships with individuals, families, carers, groups, communities and others.

This chapter will also help you achieve the following key social work benchmarks (Quality Assurance Agency for Higher Education, 2008):

- An ability to use this knowledge and understanding to engage in effective relationships with service users and carers.
- Demonstrate habits of critical reflection on their performance and take responsibility for modifying action in light of this.

Introduction

Trevithick (2005, p222) provides the following simple definition of negotiation: *achieving some form of agreement or understanding*. Although this definition does not suggest the potential complexity of the negotiating process, it does indicate the extent to which negotiation is part and parcel of our everyday lives. Certainly, negotiation appears to be integral to social work practice. However, it could be argued that, because negotiation is so embedded within the activity of social work, it is taken for granted. There are some texts which specifically focus on negotiation in health and social care, for example Fletcher (1998); yet, in many social work skills textbooks, it is noticeable that discussion of negotiation skills is frequently incorporated, or subsumed, within chapters on assessment or care planning. This is in sharp contrast to texts relating to business, where negotiation is given a far greater profile.

An instruction manual approach to negotiation, which breaks down the skills of human interaction into simple, sequential steps, may not be appropriate for social work: arguably, the subtlety and fluidity of the processes of communication are not so easily simplified. Consequently, although this chapter will explore some models of negotiation, we will attempt to avoid you having to memorise sequential techniques that they may struggle to recall in real-life practice situations. Instead, this chapter will refer to models of negotiation that draw upon those skills and qualities with which social workers are already familiar. The chapter will also address negotiation in situations of conflict, ethical issues and dilemmas, and explore how the evolution of models of self-directed support may affect the way negotiation is performed.

Negotiation skills: the practice context

Social work practitioners employ negotiation skills in interactions with:

- people who use services, carers and others who provide assistance and support;
- managers, colleagues and other staff within the practitioner's organisation;
- service providers;
- other professionals/organisations.

The authors have noted that students on qualifying and post-qualifying courses most typically refer to negotiation in the context of their direct work with service users and when attempting to secure resources. Of course, in care management roles, the two are frequently inextricably linked. Interestingly, recent research suggests that service users value practitioners who can act as 'go-betweens'; negotiating and mediating between the service user and the local authority (Manthorpe, et al., 2008). However, practitioners often report feeling ethically compromised and inadequate when negotiating to meet the needs of service users within the constraints of limited resources. Therefore, it is important to stress that better negotiating skills, on their own, cannot enable practitioners to bridge the gap between the legitimate demands of service users and the inadequate resources that are available to meet them. Nevertheless, practitioners who develop their negotiating skills are likely to improve their effectiveness when working on behalf of service users. Similarly, social workers who enhance their skills may well feel more confident and capable.

It may be possible to assume that standardised eligibility criteria, and procedural approaches to decision-making, rather undermine the practitioner's influence upon the allocation of resources. However, there is evidence to suggest that practitioners can and do exercise discretion and professional autonomy in their interactions with service users (Evans and Harris, 2004) and that skills and knowledge of the worker do make a difference in securing resources (Newton and Browne, 2008). Of course this raises ethical and political issues, if service users are effectively in competition with one another for resources, and if access to these resources is determined less by individual need than by the negotiating ability of the practitioner. This debate is largely beyond the scope of this chapter, which does not seek to give practitioners an ethically questionable, competitive advantage in their professional interactions.

However, we acknowledge that social workers practise in the world as it is, not as it should be, and recognise that it is legitimate for social workers to try to maximise the support which they can secure for service users. Consequently, practitioners will probably wish to enhance their negotiating effectiveness on behalf of service users, and for reasons of professional competence.

ACTIVITY *7.1*

On a scale of 1–5 (with 5 being the highest score), how would you assess your negotiation skills?
Does the effectiveness of your skills vary in different contexts?
Now consider what factors need to be present for your skills to be particularly effective.

Comment

It is likely that you will have concluded that how well you negotiate varies according to a number of factors. Some people may feel quite comfortable negotiating on behalf of someone else, but less capable when they feel they are asking for something for themselves; for example, you may find yourself to be an assertive advocate for service users but feel far less capable of negotiating a pay rise for yourself (of course, the converse could be true). Similarly, as a social work practitioner, you may find yourself negotiating, on behalf of your agency, for a course of action that perhaps is uncomfortable. This discomfort may affect your ability to empathise with the individual with whom you are negotiating; you may find yourself in an entrenched position and saying things that, upon reflection, you may not agree with. This is a relatively common occurrence in potentially conflictual situations. Diplomats, police officers and, probably, most parents would recognise the social worker's experience of situations which start out as a reasonable and promising discussion, then quickly and bewilderingly escalate into heated argument.

Conflictual situations often elicit strong emotion. Therefore, it is wise to acknowledge the emotional element of negotiation, since emotion is an integral feature of human interaction. Anxiety, frustration and anger are likely to have an impact upon any negotiation, as will emotions like sympathy and a sense of guilt. Similarly, it is likely that if you feel anxious, unsure of your facts and are fearful of 'losing', your negotiating ability may be severely inhibited. These issues will be specifically addressed in this chapter.

CASE STUDY

Sarah is employed by a care management team working with disabled people. She is very passionate about her job and is committed to what she calls getting the best for the people I work with. *However, she is frequently frustrated by the negotiations she undertakes on behalf of disabled people, concerning the amount of personal assistance her*

CASE STUDY *continued*

local authority is willing to fund. Even before she enters into discussions with her managers, Sarah feels stressed and anxious about 'losing'. Although she tries to find a compromise solution, she frequently finds herself feeling defensive as she is asked questions which she struggles to answer. She feels that these negotiations often end up as interrogations, where her competence, values and professional judgment are called into question. Sarah finds herself embarrassed in these discussions; especially when she is accused of not being 'realistic', or is criticised for not having followed some aspect of agency procedure. She gets anxious reporting back to the individuals she is advocating for; she tries to put an encouraging slant on disappointing decisions, but gets upset when the individuals she is working with appear to perceive her as an unthinking functionary of the social services department. Sarah frequently feels that she is trying to reconcile the impossible, with her role reduced to that of a mouthpiece for decisions she does not always believe in.

ACTIVITY 7.2

What steps do you think Sarah could take to address some of the difficulties highlighted in the case study?

Comment

It is relatively easy to empathise with Sarah's experience. Her situation is reminiscent of the ambiguous and contradictory position occupied by many social work practitioners: attempting to advocate for service users, while simultaneously being the representative of an organisation that is restricting access to resources. Of course, these professional anxieties and dilemmas are real for front-line practitioners in a variety of public service agencies (Lipsky, 1980). However, it is arguable that the social work profession claims a particularly strong commitment to the principles of anti-oppressive practice. Consequently, the reflective practitioner can hardly fail to notice if there is a gap between these principles and the apparent realities of practice.

Numerous studies identify the extent to which the priorities of social care agencies have been driven by resource constraint (Postle, 2002; Gorman and Postle, 2003). These resource concerns add legitimacy to the restructuring and remodelling of social work practice as an administrative activity. This construction of practice seems to place limited value on interpersonal skills, can seem at odds with the concerns and priorities of service users and frequently conflicts with the professional values of practitioners (Dustin, 2007). This has important implications for practitioners: ambiguity, contradiction and confusion in professional roles can be a major source of stress (Handy, 2005). Similarly, Ferguson and Lavalette (2004) argue that the increasing bureaucratisation of social work has resulted in social workers experiencing their work as a series of 'alien' practices, over which they have little control. This can lead to stress, poor morale and burn-out.

The managerial and bureaucratic remodelling of social work practice is conceived as a direct challenge to notions of professional autonomy. Coincidentally, but for different reasons, many in the disabled people's movement are apparently hostile towards the social work profession. Here, this hostility is born of the interference, insensitivity and abuses of power; perpetrated both by individual workers and social work agencies (Beresford, 2008). In these circumstances, it is not surprising that Sarah may feel so unhappy. Yet, research with service users reveals that the following social work skills and qualities are valued:

- commitment to social rather than medical models;
- ability and willingness to listen and be non-judgmental;
- willingness to advocate on behalf of service users;
- relationship with the worker based on genuineness and honesty;
- human qualities of warmth, empathy and respect.

(DHSS, 1985; Beresford, et al., 2005; Branfield, et al., 2006)

In the next section on negotiating styles, you may wish to consider whether the case study gave any clues about the negotiating styles which may have been adopted by Sarah and her managers.

Negotiating styles

Shell (2006) identifies five negotiation styles:

- competitive;
- avoiding;
- accommodating;
- compromising;
- collaborative.

He suggests that individuals may have a strong preference for a particular approach or approaches. However, he argues that individuals may adopt differing approaches according to the situation. Similarly, awareness of one's own preferred styles, their strengths and weaknesses, can enable the individual to be more adept in negotiating scenarios.

Shell (2006) identifies that some individuals enjoy the competition of negotiation; they literally 'play to win'. In employing a competing style, negotiators may well secure an initial perception of victory. However, this may be to the detriment of the relationship with the other party. In a profession which places a high premium on the establishment and maintenance of positive relationships, the risks of an over-reliance on a competing style are clear.

A competitive approach may be favoured by individuals who wish to establish and maintain control. These individuals can seem strong and intimidating, particularly if occupying a supervisory position. Yet the impression of control and confidence can be illusory. Insecurity and anxiety may be revealed by a lack of willingness to depart from a narrowly defined agenda. Similarly, a refusal to acknowledge perspectives, other than one's own, can be masked by a claim to rationality; a dismissal of others' arguments as being irrelevant; a belief that the other party is over-emotional and insufficiently objective. Gabriel (1998) suggests that the fear of losing control of situations leads many managers to disguise their uncertainty behind an illusion of objectivity and emotional detachment.

Perhaps diametrically opposed to the competing style is the avoiding style; many practitioners may have witnessed this in action. Avoiders are not confident and dislike negotiation; they are more likely to skirt around potentially contentious or conflictual issues. Unlike those who enjoy a competitive style of negotiation, avoiders may appear to place a high value on positive relationships. Unfortunately, this can be to the detriment of the relationship if a degree of dishonesty is present. When social work practice has gone wrong, the subsequent inquiries have often highlighted the extent to which anxiety, about damaging the relationship with service users, has led to practitioners not addressing areas of concern. In fact, important work by Dale et al. (1986) suggests that a practitioner's need to be liked may result in them being insufficiently assertive, leading to dangerous practice. Of course, this is interesting when examined in the context of research which suggests that, even where conflictual relationships existed between service users and social work agencies, service users respected practitioners who were 'honest' and 'genuine' (DHSS, 1985). Perhaps it is sobering to acknowledge that both these pieces of work are over 20 years old; yet the lessons have still not fully permeated social work practice.

Shell (2006) identifies accommodators as individuals who value relationships and enjoy problem-solving. The inherent risk of this approach is that the individual can be too accommodating and may feel taken advantage of; this feeling may be particularly acute following an encounter with another individual who adopts a more competitive style. Similarly, compromisers may too readily give concessions that may be regretted later. However, where there is fundamental disagreement between parties, willingness to compromise, at least to a certain degree, is probably essential to avoid deadlock.

A collaborative approach appears to be attractive within social work practice: a high value is placed upon empathising with the perspectives of others and working out complex issues together. However, there is a risk that negotiation can get bogged down in the complexity of detail, if an attempt is made to reach a consensus on a myriad issues, where there may be fundamental disagreement. Occasionally, parties may have to 'agree to disagree' and accept that not all issues can be resolved by consensus.

ACTIVITY 7.3

Consider a recent practice situation or experience and reflect upon the negotiating style that you adopted.
What negotiation style do you think the other individual employed?
How successful was the negotiation?

ACTIVITY 7.3 *continued*

Did the other individual's, or your own, style of negotiation enhance or inhibit the process?

What could you have done differently that might have improved the outcome?

Comment

In dynamic and fluid practice situations it is frequently difficult to adhere to fixed models and methods (Payne, 2007). A positive feature of the Shell (2006) framework is that it provides sufficiently overarching concepts that can be witnessed in practice. Hopefully, you will have been able to identify your own and others' preferred styles of negotiation and the practice implications of these. In the next section we will explore a sequential model, where Shell (2006) provides a structure for understanding the negotiating process itself.

The stages of negotiation

In the introduction to this chapter, suspicions were highlighted regarding step-by-step instruction manual approaches to the complexities of real-life practice situations. Nevertheless, Shell (2006) provides some illuminating insights into the processes that occur during negotiation. It is worth exploring these and considering the extent to which they can be applied in social work practice. Shell (2006) suggests that the negotiation process can be broken down into four interdependent stages.

Preparation

In the case study involving Sarah, she felt defensive and struggled to answer questions that were asked of her. Possibly, a lack of prior preparation, allied with uncertainty about her facts, led to poor confidence and performance when negotiating. Adequate preparation is a precondition of successful negotiation. According to Shell (2006), this preparation does not only extend to the possession of factual information. Knowledge of an individual's negotiating style, alongside strengths and weaknesses, would appear to also be a prerequisite. Interestingly, Shell (2006) emphasises the necessity of acknowledging one's own value base and the values of the other party. Recognition of these seeks to avoid the emergence of intransigent negotiating positions; perhaps the result of emotional responses to the negotiating process.

Exchanging information

Shell (2006) argues that successful negotiators ask more questions than poor negotiators. The purpose of these questions is to understand the other party's views, values and anxieties. A successful negotiator aims for an empathic understanding of the other individual's perspective. Of course, this does not just involve asking questions;

active listening, and other skills used in daily practice, form the foundation of successful negotiation.

Interestingly, this aspect of Shell's model is very similar to the Exchange Model of Assessment (Smale, et al., 1993, 2000). In this model, the exchange of information between practitioner and service user, or others in the immediate support network, is important in ensuring a shared understanding of issues and differing perspectives. There are obvious parallels with the 'collaborative' style of negotiation identified by Shell (2006). He argues that a collaborative style may run the risk of contributing to negotiations getting 'bogged down' in detail and minor disagreement. Interestingly, Smale, et al. (1993) suggest that practitioners employing the exchange model may use their skills to act in various ways: as an 'honest broker'; to challenge, and confront others with their responsibilities; to not become enmeshed in the problematic relationships that may characterise the client's social situation.

Bargaining

Negotiation is often associated with bargaining; and, especially when under pressure of time, there is a tendency to 'get down to business', or 'cut to the chase'. However, Shell (2006) identifies bargaining as only one of a number of stages in the negotiating process; the success of this stage is conditional upon the success of those preceding it. It is argued that too little attention is paid to the exchanging of information. In fact, the model proposes delaying the bargaining stage for as long as possible, to ensure that there has been a comprehensive and effective discussion beforehand. The rationale is that effective information exchange allows the parties to understand each other, identify common ground and values and perhaps allow possible, previously unidentified, options or solutions to emerge.

Arguably, the concept of bargaining suggests the act of reaching compromise, giving something up to secure something else or, to use a less delicate phrase, 'horse trading'. Although this may be acceptable, practitioners need to be aware of the dangers of a form of moral relativism, where everything is open to negotiation. This may not be the case when negotiation compromises service users' rights or where the issue being discussed involves legal duties and responsibilities, for the agency or for the service user.

Closing and commitment

Once an agreement has been reached, mechanisms should be in place to ensure that the parties involved in a negotiation fully understand precisely what has been agreed; and that the record of the agreement and any actions arising from it are unambiguous. However, it is possible for both parties to come away from a negotiation with subtly, and occasionally radically, different interpretations of what was said and agreed. Pressure of time, and possibly the relief at reaching agreement, may result in insufficient attention being paid to accurate phrasing and recording the nature of the agreement.

ACTIVITY 7.4

Preparation for negotiation is vital. Using another practice experience, reflect upon the people you were negotiating with:
What difference would it have made to know more about who they were, and what they wanted?

Comment

We have already noted that the pace of much contemporary social work practice does not appear to lend itself to the development of long-term professional relationships. Consequently it can be difficult to establish the trust that can be the cornerstone of successful negotiation. However, it is probably fair to say that crisis-driven work carries its own momentum, which can make it difficult for the practitioner to slow down, think, prepare and reflect (Gilligan, 2004). We will return to this theme when discussing negotiation and self-directed support. Nevertheless, it is probably worth remembering that social workers, generally, are skilled at putting themselves in others' shoes: empathising and understanding other people's perspectives. No matter how stressed, or pushed for time, practitioners should arguably allow at least a little time to 'tune in' to the other individual/s' possible wishes, needs, anxieties and hopes (Taylor and Devine, 1993). Simple preparation like this is likely to improve the negotiating process and enhance the practitioner's confidence and sense of focus.

Ethical issues and questions for practitioners

When engaged in negotiation activities, practitioners may face a number of ethical questions and dilemmas: they may find themselves caught between the interests of service users and the demands of the organisation; their professional values may be subject to challenge and contradiction, leading to discomfort; they may be left feeling that social work practice is inherently concerned with compromise, ambiguity and doubt.

Bateman (2000) explores the links between negotiation and advocacy and asserts that not all situations are appropriate for negotiation. For example, social workers should not engage in negotiations that diminish service users' rights and legal entitlements. The General Social Care Council Code of Practice for Social Care Workers (GSCC, 2004, p4) places a duty on practitioners to *Protect the rights and promote the interests of service users and carers*. Practitioners could be seen to be in breach of their terms of registration if, for example, they contravened legislation when negotiating reduced levels of support for a service user.

Community care legislation is complex and ambiguous in the way it is interpreted (Clements and Thompson, 2007). Consequently, there is considerable scope for confusion and misinterpretation on the part of practitioners, local authorities and service users. Practitioners may seek to resort to agency procedure to resolve the questions that legal complexities generate. However, there is no guarantee that these procedures, or at least the interpretation of them at a local level, conform to the requirements of law. Therefore, a practitioner's knowledge of the legal framework in which they operate is essential to ensure that their practice conforms to the GSCC Codes of Practice. Specifically, it enables practitioners to recognise when the role of acting as a 'go-between', between service users and agencies, should not be one of negotiator, but that of advocate. In these circumstances, it may be appropriate for the practitioner to cease their own negotiating role and arrange for independent advocacy (Bateman, 2000).

Nevertheless, negotiation on principles of law should not be rejected out of hand, when the legal framework allows agencies to exercise discretion in the interpretation of their duties. Practitioners and agencies may interpret their own policies and procedures as absolutes, with little room for discretion (Dustin, 2007). However, these policies are frequently local interpretations of legislation or national policy. Arguably, a little-known and overarching legal principle is that local authorities should not 'fetter their discretion' by adopting too rigid an interpretation of law and policy, resulting in an unreasonable decision (Clements and Thompson, 2007).

It must be recognised that it can be very difficult and uncomfortable for practitioners to occupy the position of advocate or negotiator on behalf of service users. If the practitioner is in an oppositional role to the demands of their organisation, they can find themselves marginalised; and, their opinions discounted. Hawkins and Shohet (2007) discuss some of the forms this may take in those organisations which are characterised by an authoritarian or defensive culture. Similarly, they argue that organisations, if primarily concerned with administrative efficiency, often focus on tasks to the exclusion of personal relations. This focus does not just extend to the relationship between the employee and the organisation, but to the way in which work with service users is defined and carried out. Beresford (2008) discusses the way in which social care has become increasingly defined in terms of measurable tasks and outcomes, to the exclusion of process. Yet, service users' own definitions of quality in public services highlight the importance of 'how' the work is done, not just 'what' is done.

These issues are integral to the ethical basis of negotiation in social care: if the practitioner conceives of themselves primarily as a gatekeeper for scarce resources then they may embark on the negotiating process with a particular, procedural mindset. Specifically, they may pre-empt the outcome of the exchanging information stage of negotiation by filtering anything that is said by the other party through their internalised and restrictive definition of the agency's eligibility criteria. This procedural approach may be oppressive and severely restrict the opportunity for free discussion and the identification of creative solutions to problems (Thompson, 2000).

CASE STUDY

Danny is a busy hospital-based social worker. He enjoys the work, but finds it difficult to manage his workload. This primarily consists of arranging the discharge of older people. The work is highly pressurised and potentially conflictual: Danny frequently feels that he

---

> ### CASE STUDY *continued*
>
> *has to negotiate and mediate between the desires of the ward staff and the needs of older people and their families. He feels under pressure to arrange a quick discharge; yet he is aware that it can take time to make potentially life-changing decisions. The nature of the work results in Danny not necessarily having time to develop a relationship with the individuals with whom he is working, before he is engaged in negotiating their discharge from hospital. When Danny tries to support service users to take time to reach a decision, he feels that he is criticised by the hospital for working too slowly and for contributing to the 'bed-blocking' crisis.*

Comment

The case study illustrates some of the tensions previously discussed. The following research summary highlights some of the wider problems that can arise from the local day-to-day conflicts between the principles of anti-oppressive practice and the organisational pressures of resource constraint.

> ### RESEARCH SUMMARY
>
> *Research by CSCI (2004, 2005) explored the process of hospital discharge. The research concluded that the process was largely driven by the need to release beds to allow further admissions. There was some evidence to suggest that patients were pushed into making complex and profoundly important decisions when they were unwell. Similarly, discussions and negotiations often took place in a hospital ward environment where it was difficult to make these decisions; the absence of privacy being not least of the concerns. Consequently, individuals may have agreed to courses of action which they later regretted; possibly leading to inappropriate admissions to long-term care.*

Negotiation in situations of conflict

Negotiating where there is conflict can be particularly stressful and challenging. The work of Ury (1991) provides some useful ideas for those social work practitioners who may be approaching a negotiation situation with some trepidation. Central to this model is recognition of one's own and others' emotions. Specifically, Ury (1991) suggests that, when confronted by difficult situations, individuals may get angry and strike back, break off the discussion and withdraw or give in to others' demands. None of these alternatives is likely to lead to an effective resolution.

Ury (1991) cautions against negotiating when angry; his first suggestion is: *Don't react: Go to the balcony.* This requires the negotiator to be aware of themselves, and how they may be perceived; be aware of what makes them angry and attempt to control their own emotional reactions; try to observe dispassionately the other party's tactics and the other party's motivation. Fletcher (1998) identifies that it is easy to mirror aggression with aggression but, as Ury points out, this merely sustains the confrontation. It may also be exactly what the other party wishes; it enables them to deflect attention from the central issue of concern. Consequently, Ury recommends taking time to *go to the balcony*; to pause, take a break, review the discussion and not be pressurised or bullied into making a concession that may be later regretted.

Ury (1991) is clear that arguments are unproductive, not least because the heightened emotional content of the confrontation is likely to polarise the negotiation into a battle of winning and losing. Individuals are less likely to reach a negotiated agreement if they perceive offering concessions as losing. Consequently, instead of taking an oppositional stance, Ury recommends *stepping to the side.* In essence, Ury recommends those skills that are familiar to social workers: the skills of active listening, to demonstrate your awareness of the other party's point of view, their difficulties and their feelings. Effective negotiators should never be afraid to apologise if appropriate and, as Shell (1999) recommends, ask questions.

Questions are also key to the third element of Ury's model, which focuses on reframing problems or sources of disagreement. Asking 'why' questions helps clarify the other party's interests, and it may be possible to reframe firm positions as aspirations. 'What if' questions help identify possible solutions, in a hypothetical way, which may not be perceived as a direct challenge to the other party's entrenched position. Underlying this use of questions is Ury's suggestion that solutions to problems can frequently be found by focusing on the shared interests of the parties, rather than what divides them.

The fourth and fifth elements of the model focus on not backing the other party into a corner. Ury (1991) argues that the negotiator should allow the other party to retreat, make concessions, or reach agreement without losing face. Drawing on the words of an ancient Chinese general, Sun Tzu, Ury suggests that negotiators should not push, but should *build your opponent a golden bridge to retreat across*. The fifth stage of negotiation comes into play if the other party refuses to reach agreement. Again, Ury cautions against escalation and displays of power: it may be possible to force an agreement, but it is likely to lack the commitment of both parties and may not last. Ury recommends using questions to ensure that the other party considers what could happen if an agreement is not reached: what will the consequences be? What will they do? What do they think you will do? Even if it is possible to secure a 'victory', achieving a lasting agreement through negotiation is recommended; this may require assistance from a third party.

Negotiation in the context of self-directed support: the practitioner's role

The government's 'personalisation agenda' promises a radical shift in the way in which social care and personal support are defined and delivered. The success of this transformation is premised upon changes in professional and organisational cultures. These are seen as integral to a necessary transfer of power away from professionals, and formal organisations, and into the hands of service users. This poses many questions for the role of practitioners in this new environment, not least in relation to their role in negotiation. Arguably, negotiating in the context of self-directed support involves all the previously mentioned issues. However, the following themes highlighted by Clements (2008) are also likely to be characteristic of the negotiating process.

- Self-directed support necessarily involves negotiating with people whose conception of the pattern of support they want may not fit with what the practitioner feels is needed or appropriate.

- People may choose to be assisted by others whom the practitioner would not necessarily choose; this may require managing safeguarding and protection concerns in partnership with the client, instead of as a professional expert.

- Practitioners may find it difficult to relinquish control and see the client as someone who may be taking major responsibilities themselves; for example, being an employer rather than someone to whom services are given.

- The evolving pattern of policy, practice and innovation may leave practitioners unsure of their roles; negotiation in this context will probably be more complex and less comfortable.

ACTIVITY 7.5

To what extent do you think your professional role may change in the context of the development of self-directed support?
How might this challenge or modify your professional and personal values?
To what extent do you feel the culture of your organisation will enable it to adapt to new ways of working?

Comment

With regard to direct payments, the attitudes of practitioners have been cited as barriers to change (Clark and Spafford, 2001). Similarly, the social work tradition of 'doing and giving' (Henwood and Hudson, 2007, p19) may not sit comfortably with a less directive, arguably less powerful, practitioner role. However, Harrop (2008, p2) highlights the difficulties in changing organisational cultures; she argues that there is a danger of trying to *graft good ideas onto structures and assumptions that are problematic*. Furthermore, she considers that organisational and professional cultures are often more resistant to change than is recognised.

In this context it is interesting to consider the ideas framed by Gilligan (2004). He draws on the work of Harris (1993) to suggest that a good deal of social work practice can be understood through the metaphor of the 'fire brigade': practice that is crisis-driven, dramatic, and characterised by notions of 'rescue' and the omnipotent practitioner. This approach is not conducive to developing a partnership that acknowledges and supports service user strengths and self-determination. In fact, practitioners need *to temper any assumption that change begins and ends with anything they do* (Gilligan, 2004, p98).

Although Gilligan primarily refers to child care practice, his observations do appear to have some wider resonance; arguably organisational and professional approaches to risk demonstrate many of the features of the 'fire brigade' metaphor. However, the philosophy that underpins self-directed support challenges the defensive approaches to risk that are characteristic of much professional practice (Smethurst, 2008). In fact McLaughlin (2007) argues that the government's personalisation agenda is philosophically inconsistent with its other protective and defensive policies towards 'vulnerable' people.

It is evident that the personalisation agenda is likely to result in practitioners having to negotiate in situations of ambiguity, where philosophy, policy and organisational practice may be inconsistent or contradictory. Nevertheless, it is to be hoped that, as the philosophy of self-directed support becomes more established, it should and could provide practitioners with a way of using negotiation to work positively with service users. We must hope that the exchange model and the social model of disability will finally make the transition from being aspirations to the cornerstones of everyday practice.

CHAPTER SUMMARY

Negotiation is an integral, but often underexplored, feature of social work practice. Management and business literature provides a wealth of negotiating models and techniques. However, their application in social work practice may be limited.

Nevertheless, the exploration of models of negotiation does highlight many similarities with accepted good practice in social work; for example, the principles of effective information sharing in negotiation bear many similarities to the key aspects of the exchange model of assessment.

Professional and organisational cultures have a major impact on the autonomy of the practitioner, and the nature of the negotiating relationship with service users and other professionals.

Emerging models of self-directed support provide opportunities for practitioners to use their negotiating skills constructively. However, for the practitioner, role tensions may arise if the philosophy of personalisation remains at odds with dominant organisational philosophies and practice.

RTHER
ADING

Fletcher, K (1998) *Negotiation for health and social service professionals.* London: Jessica Kingsley.
A useful introduction to negotiation in the context of social care.

Hawkins, P and Shohet, R (2006) *Supervision in the helping professions* (3rd edition).
Maidenhead: Open University Press.
This book provides a valuable exploration of negotiation in the area of supervision, with frameworks for considering the issues and improving practice.

Shell, R (2006) *Bargaining for advantage: Negotiating strategies for reasonable people.* New York: Penguin Books.
A good introduction to individual roles and styles in negotiation.

PART 3
PROFESSIONAL ACCOUNTABILITY
AND COMPETENCE

Chapter 8

Case recording and report-writing skills
Gill Constable

A C H I E V I N G   A   S O C I A L   W O R K   D E G R E E

This chapter will help you to meet the following National Occupational Standards:

Key Role 5: Manage and be accountable, with supervision and support, for your own social work practice within your organisation.

- Manage, present and share records and reports.
  - Maintain accurate, complete, accessible, and up-to-date records and reports.
  - Provide evidence for judgments and decisions.
  - Implement legal and policy framework for access to records and reports.
  - Share records with individuals, families, carers, groups and communities.

This chapter will also help you achieve the following key social work benchmarks (Quality Assurance Agency for Higher Education, 2008):

- Communication skills
  - Write accurately and clearly in styles adapted to the audience, purpose and context of the communication.
  - Present conclusions verbally and on paper, in a structured form, appropriate to the audience for which these have been prepared.

Introduction

In this chapter we are going to focus on writing and its importance for social work as a profession, as well as for people that use services and carers, but to start off we will reflect on two quotes that you may well hear repeated while you are on placement:

> *I didn't become a social worker because I wanted to be a typist or a computer programmer. I want to work with people, not waste my time in front of a machine.*
> (Comment from a social care assessor)

> *My staff are good at what they do, not what they write down.*
> (A Director of Social Services)

> (DoH, 1999d, pp2 and 29)

These were comments made to the Department of Health Inspectors during a review of seven local authorities' social services departments inspecting their case recording procedures and practice. We will begin by thinking about writing, as an aspect of communication (see Chapter 2), and the value that society places on it, and the different types of writing that social workers do. It will be positioned within the ethical and value base of social work. Confidentiality, sharing and access to records will be discussed. Linkages will be made with the academic work you are required to do at university, and how those skills can be transferred to your practice in placement. Some advice will be given to assist you in the development of effective writing skills, so you can view writing as an ally in your personal and professional development.

What is the purpose of writing?

Thompson (2003) states that writing is a powerful activity, which is demonstrated by the law, policy, guidance, and legal documents such as birth certificates and wills being written down. It is the method in modern societies by which events are recorded. Writing is a form of communication and it endures, unlike the spoken word. The skills of listening, speaking and observing non-verbal communication such as body language are core to social work, but so are well-developed writing skills. Healy and Mulholland (2007, p11) identify the differences between speech and writing as follows.

- Writing stands alone and cannot be enhanced by non-verbal communication, unlike speech.

- Speaking involves other people unlike reading, which is usually a solitary activity. It is important that writing is clear, carefully structured and the reader is guided through the process.

- The writer does not know who might read the document, and therefore areas that need clarification should be anticipated, as people cannot ask questions.

- Written documents allow the reader to reflect on their contents and re-read them. This is not the case with the spoken word.

- Writing is permanent and may be referred to in the future.

CASE STUDY

Aaban had come to the United Kingdom seeking asylum when he was 22 years old. He had witnessed violence and experienced trauma as an adolescent. Within six months of his arrival in the UK he became mentally unwell. Aaban agreed to admission to the local psychiatric hospital for assessment and treatment. He was described as fearful, agitated and very confused. After a couple of weeks Aaban began to feel calmer, but had virtually no memory of his first six months in the UK. Aaban found this confusing and it created anxiety for him. He was unable to fully engage with Sophia, the social worker who was planning his discharge from hospital with him.

CASE STUDY *continued*

Sophia explained to Aaban that unfortunately she could not 'fill in the gaps' for him, as the social worker who had been involved in his admission had recently left to go travelling, and writing up his interviews was not his strong point. Sophia agreed with Aaban that she would record their meetings and prior to the end of each meeting she would summarise what they had agreed. Additionally she told Aaban how he could access his case file, and reassured him by saying that from this time forward there would be a comprehensive written recording following each of their meetings. Sophia was surprised at how grateful Aaban was.

Comment

Imagine how you might feel if you could not remember a significant part of your life. This could include details about your family and friends, as well information about your life history, skills and simple preferences such as the things that you enjoy doing. You would probably feel very relieved if someone was able to help you regain your memory, and put you in touch with your family and friends. If you were told that this crucial person who could link you with the past had failed to record any of your details, had left their job and was not contactable, how might you feel? Sophie explained to Aaban the boundaries that surrounded the maintenance and use of records including his entitlement to access them. This is a significant point, as in oppressive political regimes records can be used as evidence against people, and therefore it was important for Aaban to understand his rights to see information about his life.

For some people who use services, written records that are compiled by social workers may be the main or only source of information about significant events in their life (DoH, 1999d). This highlights how important it is to maintain quality records. Poor records can also lead to:

- inappropriate action being taken, or no action;
- complaints being made that might result in litigation (Thompson, 2003).

RESEARCH SUMMARY

What we can learn from child protection case records?
Between 1973 and 1994 the quality of written records was criticised in the report findings of 45 public inquiries into the death of a child where social workers were involved. Key findings were:

- *scarcity of information;*

- *inaccurate information;*

- *no statement about who was seen on the visit;*

- *information not collated or linked together.*

(Munro, 1998, p94)

Comment

These findings suggest that the social workers had not developed a systematic process to record information. Since Munro completed this research, both children's and adults' services in the statutory sector have sought to improve the design of case files, so information is easier to access. When you are on placement, have a look at some case files, and assess the quality of the recording against the findings of Munro's research. Are there differences between social workers and, if you were allocated the case, would you feel confident that you have all the information that you need?

Look at the findings of the Commission for Social Care Inspection (CSCI), soon to be replaced by the Care Quality Commission, for the local authority where you live either for a particular service or the council overall on their website. It is CSCI's responsibility to inspect and regulate all social care services. When they inspected services for people with learning difficulties on the Isle of Wight (2005), they commented that not all service uses had had an annual review of whether the service was still meeting their needs, neither was it clear if people had been sent copies of their review. Files did not always show the rationale for managers' decisions, nor was there evidence as to how risks were being managed (CSCI website, 2008).

Defining the types of written communication that social workers do

We will now consider the type of writing that social workers do.

> **ACTIVITY 8.1**
>
> *List all the different types of written communication that social workers use.*

Comment

This is dependent on the organisation for which social workers work and the purpose of the writing, which will also impact on the detail and length of the writing. Thompson (2002, pp109, 112) identifies the following types of communication used by social workers.

- Telephone messages. It is important that these are written down and dated, stating the full name of the person, concise details of the message, telephone number to ring back and the name of the person who took the message.

- Text messages. This may not be a preferred method of communication but can be very useful in an emergency situation when the mobile signal is poor. A disadvantage is that text language can obscure rather than clarify meaning.

- Letters to people who use services, other professionals and external organisations. They should follow a structure, be clear and concise.

- Memos are used when communicating in a formal manner with a manager or another team or department within the same organisation.

- Email used within an organisation and with other agencies. They are not appropriate for complex and detailed information. Some disadvantages are that they can be sent or read quickly, which may lead to misunderstandings, and can be sent off sometimes without being checked. Additionally they are often overused, which does cause stress if people have lots of emails to read. They can be used to 'cover your back' by supplying information about a case to another worker or manager. This is not appropriate or safe social work practice. The positives of emails are that they are quick and easy to use, and assist in the setting up of appointments and meetings, as a group of people can be sent the one email.

- Reports may be required internally, for example in the implementation of the Safeguarding Adults' Procedures, or formally requested by an external agency such as a mental health tribunal.

- Referral is a request for an assessment or service; for example a general practitioner requesting assistance to be provided to one of their patients.

- Assessments. Many agencies have standard assessment templates for social workers and other professionals to complete. The development of self-directed or personalised care for people who use services means that, increasingly, social workers will be supporting service users and carers to develop the skills to assess their own needs (see Chapter 4).

- Care plans set out how the person's needs are to be met, that is their health, emotional, spiritual, cultural, educational, leisure and employment needs (see Chapter 4).

- Case recording sheets. Time, dates, people seen and setting down the work that has been achieved with the person who uses services.

- Process recording is detailed writing about the process of the interview which includes verbal and non-verbal communication, and the social worker's reflection and observations on self and others.

- Review documents are used when the person's care plan is reassessed to see if it still meets their needs (see Chapter 4).

- Summaries are completed if a specific piece of work has been achieved, when a case is transferred to another worker or the case is closed. The summary sets out the objectives of the involvement, current situation, what has been achieved and if further work is required or expected.

- Information may be provided about services to prospective recipients or carers.

- Service specifications, contracts or service-level agreements are developed when a service has been purchased; they detail the cost, type and quality of the provision.

Moon (1999b) describes the importance of writing to develop critical thinking and reflective skills.

- Writing slows us down and requires us to concentrate.

- It enables us to organise our thinking and feelings.

- It gives us structure and control so we can set about identifying and prioritising issues.

- It can enable our understanding to be enhanced.

- It enables us to problem-solve.

- It supports us to link our thoughts with previous and present experience and knowledge, which we can use in the future.

Social workers need to develop case-recording skills to ensure that they can write effectively in a manner that is proportionate to the needs of the case. So we will now consider case recording in some detail.

Case recording

Case recording is a core activity for social workers. We have considered the importance of accurate and concise writing as a component of social work. If we specifically consider case recording, its purpose is to:

- provide information about and for people who use services;

- provide clarity about the situation and needs of the person who uses services;

- provide information for other professionals including inspectors;

- provide evidence that the policies and procedures of the agency have been followed;

- demonstrate that legal requirements are met, and good quality information is given to the courts when required;

- provide evidence as to how decisions were made;

- show evidence of good practice and that the agency is consistent in its response and methods used to assist people, which may be required if a complaint is made or an insurance claim submitted to the agency;

- provide information that supports the planning and development of services, as well as statistical information that is useful to the agency that supports policy development and the allocation of funds, for example the ethnic origin, age and needs of people accessing services;

- enable managers to audit the quality of work, and identify training and development requirements.

Below is an example of case recording which is concise and has summarised events.

CASE STUDY

18 March 2008. Mrs Smith was visited by Edwina Shaw (Community Nurse) at 11.00 a.m. Mrs Smith was undressed, confused and wandering in the garden. Mrs Smith's daughter Susan Edwards was contacted. Dr Frazer (GP) made an emergency visit and made arrangements for admission to Homefield District Hospital for assessment (Elm Ward). Mrs Smith was accompanied by her daughter Susan Edwards. Jodie Johnston (Student Social Worker) to liaise with the hospital Social Work Team on Monday regarding discharge planning.

Alison DuPont, Duty Social Worker

Comment

This is a very brief summation of the events leading to Mrs Smith's admission to hospital. In particular, note that Alison DuPont has identified the names and roles of the people involved, so that anyone could read this recording and be clear who was involved, and the whereabouts of Mrs Smith. She has indicated what action Jodie Johnston needs to take.

The ethical value base of writing as a social worker

Healy and Mulholland (2007, p14) state:

> *You should always try to represent yourself in your writing as thoughtful, objective, experienced, and careful about what you communicate.*

This is a useful maxim to follow. Writing should be underpinned by the professional role and responsibilities, processes and value base of the profession. Included within this is confidentiality. Carers and service users need to be advised that information that may indicate that they are at risk of harm, or other people are at risk, will be passed on by the social worker. Assurance should be given that information is kept confidential, and will not be exchanged casually with other people. It should be explained that information is gathered on behalf of the agency employing the social worker, and records are kept. Consent must be sought to pass non- high-risk information to other professionals where appropriate: for example, to request that an occupational therapist assesses a person with physical disabilities to enhance their mobility within their home.

People who use services are entitled to access their records under the Data Protection Act 1998 and agencies have policies and procedures in place to enable this to happen.

The Data Protection Act 1998

There are eight principles that underpin the Act and social workers should be mindful of these as they record information. Information that is from a third party recorded on case files requires that person's consent to access it.

1. Personal data shall be processed fairly and lawfully.

2. Personal data shall be obtained only for one or more specified and lawful purposes, and shall not be further processed in any manner incompatible with that purpose or those purposes.

3. Personal data shall be adequate, relevant and not excessive in relation to the purpose or purposes for which they are processed.

4. Personal data shall be accurate and, where necessary, kept up to date.

5. Personal data processed for any purpose or purposes shall not be kept for longer than is necessary for that purpose or those purposes.

6. Personal data shall be processed in accordance with the rights of data subjects under this Act.

7. Appropriate technical and organisational measures shall be taken against unauthorised or unlawful processing of personal data and against accidental loss or destruction of, or damage to, personal data.

8. Personal data shall not be transferred to a country or territory outside the European Economic Area unless that country or territory ensures an adequate level of protection for the rights and freedoms of data subjects in relation to the processing of personal data.

When social workers are recording information they need to be aware that a number of people might read it, and should learn to *communicate sensitively* (Thompson, 2003, p33). The tone of the writing and the language should be respectful and formal, as language can reinforce oppressive racist, sexist and homophobic attitudes and negative stereotypes of disabled people. It is important to reflect on the choice of words; for example, can you detect any difficulties with these statements?

> *The gentleman that was accused of sexually abusing the young man at the employment project denied it.*

> *The lady doctor was popular with the social workers in the local team, as she was supportive towards the carers of her older patients.*

The terms 'gentleman' and 'lady' are not neutral: they connote certain attributes and suggest evaluative attitudes on the part of the writer. It is preferable to use descriptive and precise language – in these examples this would be 'man' and 'female'. Although of course 'man' or 'female' or 'male' and 'woman' are also indicators of social constructions and stereotypes, so all language needs to be handled sensitively.

Forms of discourse

There are four forms of discourse that people use in speech (Healy and Mulholland, 2007, p80) although sometimes these are combined.

- Narrative form – speaking as if telling a story.

- Descriptive form – describing the people and actions in terms of how they impacted on the speaker rather than what actually happened.

- Argument form – the person presents what they want and why.

- Statement form – this is a clear description of the situation and the difficulties. The person is able to identify the outcome they want.

CASE STUDY

Precious is a social worker in a team for older people with mental health needs. On Monday morning Mrs Smith's son Ed arrives at the office with his mother. The following happens:

I've had it, Mum is so depressed and confused. We can't cope, the wife is threatening to leave me, and the kids are fed up. (Ed's eyes fill up) She's incontinent. (Ed looks at Mrs Smith)

You've got to do something – it's rubbish what you provide, she needs more than a care worker visiting three times a day – they don't always come. (Ed becomes angry, his voice becomes raised and he stares at Precious) My step-father is a waste of space. He might be old and frail but I could hang for him. He's neither use nor ornament, drinks her pension and leaves her in a mess all day. Look either you help and get her into a home, or I'm leaving her at the hospital. Get it? (Ed looks threatening)

Mrs Smith remains silent throughout the interview; her face expresses extreme anxiety.

ACTIVITY 8.2

What do you think was Ed's preferred form of discourse?

Comment

Ed's preferred discourse form is argument. He has come to the office to see Precious with a clear outcome in mind and reasons to support this. Case recording has to be written in the statement form of discourse, irrespective of the person's preferred form of discourse. It must identify the issues clearly.

Facts, opinions, hearsay, access and confidentiality

Pritchard (2007, pp284, 285), in her writing about adult abuse, states that recording should give the nature and source of the information. It is important to separate out facts, opinions and hearsay, as well as understanding the concept of confidentiality and people's entitlement to access records kept about them. This is relevant when working with all people who use services and carers. Figure 8.1 shows these key concepts that you should be able to identify when you review your writing. Read the following case study and then answer the questions with reference to the diagram.

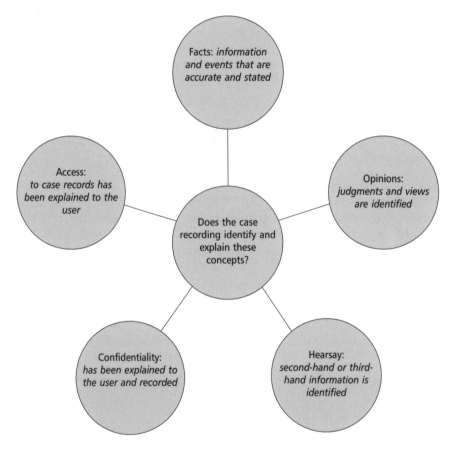

Figure 8.1 Five concepts in social work writing

CASE STUDY

Sylvia was working in a rehabilitation team in the voluntary sector for people who misuse substances. She was allocated a case of a young man, Kevin, who had a long history of both alcohol and drug misuse. The previous worker had left the following transfer summary.

I have worked with Kevin over the last 18 months, he no longer appears to use drugs, just alcohol. He started misusing substances when he was 14 years old. He has spent most of his life in care and has had a number of prison sentences mainly relating to theft and possession of Class A drugs. Kevin has three children by two different girlfriends. His relationships are short term, and his interest in his children non-existent. Kevin is seen locally as unpredictable and frightening especially when he has been drinking. The boyfriend of an ex-girlfriend of Kevin's told me that most of the pubs have banned him in the town. Kevin has taken recently to being tat-tooed, probably to offset his rather feminine appearance. This makes him appear more alarming. Overall the medical team at the unit think the prognosis for Kevin is very poor and give his life expectancy as about five years. At the present time Kevin is living with a girlfriend Deb, who has one child who is under five years old. Chil-dren's Services are involved, primarily as Deb has a history of cocaine misuse. Kevin is cooperating with his community order.

ACTIVITY *8.3*

Can you identify what the facts are in this case recording?
What is opinion?
Are there examples of hearsay information?
Have issues of confidentiality and access to records been addressed?

Comment

You are provided with information but the facts are not identified. Facts are based on events that definitely happened and information that you know to be true. The infor-mation that is given lacks depth and specificity, for example we are not told Kevin's age or ethnic origin. There is no information about his children or previous partners. There is no sense of Kevin's family or social networks or employment history. We are not provided with the name of the children's services contact or the nature of the work that is taking place and so on.

If an opinion is given in case recording, it needs to be identified as such and the following two questions asked: *Whose opinion is this? Is the person qualified to assess/give an opinion?* (Pritchard, 2007, p284). We are told Kevin's life expectancy is five years, but no medical practitioner is named. It is stated that Kevin's *relation-ships are short term, and his interest in his children non-existent.* Who has made this assessment, and are they qualified to do so?

Hearsay is information that cannot be confirmed. It is said by another person, and passed on to someone else. It is *second- or third-hand information* (Pritchard, 2007, p285). An example in this case recording is: *The boyfriend of an ex-girlfriend of Kevin's told me that most of the pubs have banned him in the town.* This information is imprecise and it would be inadmissible in a court of law, but it is powerful as it implies that Kevin's behaviour can be volatile.

The issue of confidentiality and Kevin's entitlement to access his records has not been recorded. Pritchard (2007) reminds us to ask the following questions: *Who might read this record? Will they understand what I am saying?* (p285). The statement *Kevin has taken recently to being tattooed, probably to offset his rather feminine appearance. This makes him appear more alarming,* is highly judgmental and opinionated. The concepts of femininity and masculinity are socially constructed, which means they mean different things to different people and cultures over time. They can be oppressive as they implicitly conjure up images in our mind. At this point in time what is your mental image of Kevin? What impact does the use of terms like *boyfriend* and *girlfriend* have? It is understandable if you imagine Kevin to be an adolescent, as his relationships have not been given due respect. It would be more appropriate to use the term *partner*. Thompson's (2003, p33) *communication sensitivity* stresses the need to integrate anti-oppressive practice in writing. How do you think Kevin might feel if he were to read this case summary about himself and his life? We are told one positive fact about Kevin, that he is co-operating with his community order, and yet this is not expanded upon.

Focusing on strengths in recording

Social work seeks to enable and support people to achieve change in their lives, so attention should focus on what is positive, with a balanced view of challenges and negatives. We have to address this within ourselves: do you identify the strengths within people and situations, or does your focus rest on the difficulties?

Tanner and Harris (2008, p146) have developed a template that can be used to assess our writing practice in terms of whether we are using a perspective that identifies the strengths. We will use this approach in revising a small proportion of the case recording about Kevin as an example. See Table 8.1.

Has the mental image you have of Kevin changed? If it has, this is likely to be due to the additional information that you have been given, and how it has been presented. This gives a more rounded picture of Kevin. It is important to stress that focusing on strengths does not mean that risks are ignored. These should be recorded and assessed. We will now look at how these skills can be used to write reports.

Report writing

We saw earlier that Thompson (2003) stated that the capacity to write gives authority and is potentially powerful. It is disempowering not to be able to read or write. Social workers hold this power as they are required to write reports for a wide number of uses such as: to access resources, to provide information for courts, adult protection conferences, mental health review tribunals, to obtain funding from charitable bodies, to respond to complaints, and so on. Many of the skills that you have acquired at

Principles

Write so that:

- the behaviour is described rather than using judgmental statements;
- strengths rather than difficulties are emphasised;
- language is clear, concise and easy to understand without jargon.

Negative statements	More positive statements
He no longer appears to use drugs, just alcohol	Kevin is tested regularly as part of his community order, and there is no evidence that he is using drugs. Work is focused on helping Kevin to reduce his consumption of alcohol. Kevin estimates that he has reduced his consumption from 55 units to 30 units per week. He states that he no longer drinks spirits, but consumes longer drinks such as lager. He is aware that the continuation of this level of consumption will cause ill health.
He has had a number of prison sentences	Kevin has had three prison sentences in the last seven years, the longest being six months. He has not had a custodial sentence in the last two years.
Kevin is co-operating with the community order	Kevin is fully engaged in working with the project. This involves attending two groups a week, and meeting with his key worker on a fortnightly basis. To date he has not missed any appointments, and the project is now supporting Kevin to find work.

Table 8.1 Revising Kevin's transfer summary

university when writing assignments are transferable to report writing, such as the presentation of evidence to support an argument and summarising complex ideas. The same concepts are used in report writing as in case recording.

Healy and Mulholland (2007, p90) identify the importance of the following qualities.

- Reports should be objective and factual. You need to be clear about the information that you can verify. If it is second-hand information you need to state this. For example:

  Mrs Khan told me that her father-in-law was often verbally aggressive towards her. I have not witnessed this when I have visited the family. I have noticed that Mrs Khan appears wary towards her father-in-law.

  When I interviewed Mr Khan he denied that he was aggressive towards his daughter-in-law, but he appeared confused and seemed to think Mrs Khan was his manager from when he worked for an insurance company.

- Reports should be coherent and systematic in their order and structure. There are a number of ways that you can structure your report: by chronology, by significant events and by usefulness to the reader. The language used should be accessible and understandable to the subject of the report and other professionals, so avoid jargon, and explain any services or ideas that the reader/s may not understand.

- Reports should comprise essential information. Make a list of the information that is required and prioritise what the reader needs to know. Core information will include the name, gender, ethnic origin, age of the person, the range of agencies involved, family and social networks, employment details, housing and so on.

- Reports will be more influential if they are concise, to the point, contain a clear evidence-based summary and make recommendations with action attached.

CASE STUDY

Victor had recently been appointed as a newly qualified social worker in a community mental health team. He was asked by the manager to help a colleague complete a report for the Mental Health Tribunal on a young Japanese student, Kazumi, who had been compulsorily admitted to hospital, and was seeking to be discharged. The allocated social worker was on compassionate leave due to a family bereavement.

ACTIVITY 8.4

How should Victor set about this task?
How can Victor empower Kazumi?

Comment

Victor decided to undertake some research. He accessed the Mental Health Tribunal website and downloaded general information about the role and responsibilities of the Mental Health Tribunal, and the standard template for social inquiry reports. He then asked the manager if he could see good examples of other reports that social workers had completed in the team.

Victor then planned the process that he would use to gather the information. This included visits to Kazumi, reading the nursing and medical notes and case file. He also accessed information from the BBC website to find out about Japan, so that he would have some understanding of Kazumi's culture and country of origin (BBC website, 2008). He checked with Kazumi if he wanted an interpreter, and that he had an appropriate advocate and legal advice.

Victor undertook further research into the support services within the university where Kazumi was studying, as well as community provision, to determine if there were options for discharge. He ensured that he shared this with the psychiatric team in the hospital and gained their views. Victor was very mindful of the power that he had in terms of how he wrote the report, what he highlighted and the weight he gave to strengths and risk factors. He set aside sufficient time to enable Kazumi to read the report and spent time with him explaining the content and reasons for the conclusions that he had reached.

Victor's practice sought to empower Kazumi, who was detained on a compulsory order, as he advised Kazumi of his legal rights, and ensured that he received the advocacy service that he was entitled too. Victor listened carefully to Kazumi's views, and researched community options that would enable Kazumi to be safely discharged from hospital. It is always the social worker's responsibility to engage with service users through communicating sensitively (see Chapter 1).

The practice of summation and making recommendations

One criticism that is often made of case recording and report writing is that the writing can be descriptive, with little attempt to summarise the key points and make recommendations based on a sound assessment (see Chapter 4). This may be due to defensive practice where the social worker does not have confidence to make clear decisions and recommendations (Chapter 5). It was mentioned earlier that skills are transferable from writing assignments for university, where you are required to use critical analysis and argument. These are the same skills that should become routine in case recording and report writing, so appropriate action can be taken.

C H A P T E R   S U M M A R Y

If we return to the comments made by the social care assessor and director that began this chapter we can now provide clear evidence of how erroneous these comments are. The importance of developing effective and confident writing skills has now been demonstrated. We have considered the different types of writing, and the need for this to be underpinned by the ethical and value base of social work. There are strong linkages between the writing skills and research required for academic work at university, and these skills can be transferred to your practice in placement. Writing, like all aspects of social work, requires personal reflection and self-knowledge. You need to select a method of recording and report writing that provides concise, evidence-based information and recommendations that demonstrate competent and anti-oppressive practice. Writing is a powerful activity and its effective use will enhance your professional practice and personal well-being.

FURTHER READING

Healy, K and Mulholland, J (2007) *Writing skills for social workers.* London: Sage.
This is a comprehensive and accessible book for students and qualified social workers.

Thompson, N (2003) *Communication and language.* Basingstoke: Palgrave Macmillan.
This book includes all forms of communication and addresses anti-oppressive practice.

Chapter 9

Self-presentation
Gill Constable

A C H I E V I N G   A   S O C I A L   W O R K   D E G R E E

This chapter will help you to meet the following National Occupational Standards:

Key Role 6: Demonstrate professional competence in social work practice.

- Work within agreed standards of social work practice and ensure your own professional development.
  - Use professional assertiveness to justify decisions and uphold professional social work practice, values and ethics.
  - Work within the principles and values underpinning social work practice.

This chapter will also help you achieve the following key social work benchmarks (Quality Assurance Agency for Higher Education, 2008):

Skills in personal and professional development.

Honours graduates in social work should be able to:

- advance their own learning and understanding with a degree of independence;
- reflect on and modify their behaviour in the light of experience;
- manage uncertainty, change and stress in work situations;
- handle inter- and intrapersonal conflict constructively;
- understand and manage changing situations and respond in a flexible manner;
- challenge unacceptable practices in a responsible manner;
- take responsibility for their own further and continuing acquisition of knowledge and skills.

Introduction

In this chapter we will be looking at self-presentation. This is not simply about our appearance, but our behaviours, thoughts, belief systems and values that impact on how we present to ourselves and others, and what this means as a social worker. The approach that will be adopted is thinking about our development as part of a journey where our destination is to become a competent, empathic and reflective practitioner. But in some senses of course the journey never ends and the gaining of *practice wisdom* (Hardiker and Barker, 1981, p2) incrementally increases with experience. So while reading this chapter you will need to be focused on enhancing your own self-awareness, and the impact that you have on others. We will start by looking at self-identity and the concept of professionalism through exploring belief systems, and how these impact on our *metaphor of life* (Cottrell, 2003, p39). We will move on to the development of critical and analytical skills and assertive behaviour as this is empowering to us and others.

The importance of self-awareness in social work

Thompson (2005) seeks to define social work, and summarises it as the performance of statutory duties, the management of both caring for and controlling people. Social work resides between people's personal difficulties and issues that cause public concern. He states that social work can be seen as doing *society's dirty work* (p6), so it is paramount that social work is committed to social justice. The profession is underpinned by the General Social Care Council's (GSCC) National Occupational Standards and as individuals social workers are responsible for their own professional practice. The values of social work are:

- *Respect for people regardless of age, ethnicity, and need.*
- *Empowering individuals, carers, groups and communities in decisions that impact on them.*
- *Honesty about the power that social workers have, such as legal authority, and access to resources.*
- *Treating information as confidential and being clear who it needs to be shared with.*
- *Challenge discriminatory images and practices that affect individuals, families, carers, groups and communities.*
- *Ensure that the needs of individuals, groups and communities are at the centre of everything that social workers do.*

(GSCC, 2002, p4)

Thompson (2005) goes on to highlight the importance of a value base for practitioners as it provides a guide to action; a framework to understand practice; a process to determine decisions; motivation and commitment to practice. Gilbert (2005, p33) when writing about the leadership of self, states:

> *Crucial to this is whether the leader has positive values, is aware of them, can nurture them and turn them into positive behaviours.*

The link between values and behaviour is clearly stated here. Social work offers plenty of challenge. There is a fine balance between care and control within people's lives, as can be seen, for example, in safeguarding adults. How important is self-awareness in social work? Can you be a social worker during your working hours and at other times engage in activities or hold beliefs that are in contradiction to social work values?

CASE STUDY

Steve was a mature student in his first semester at university. He was generally regarded in his circle of friends as the 'funny man'. He recognised that sometimes his humour was a bit near the mark, but he always rationalised this to himself by thinking that people should 'lighten up'. Steve was genuinely surprised when challenged about his sexism by his friend Iain, when he called another female student 'Nice Legs' in the student bar.

Do you think this type of behaviour occurring socially is less of an issue than if it had taken place during teaching time, or on a social work placement?
Why do you think that Steve was surprised at being challenged by Iain?

Comment

One way to respond to this case study is to assess Steve's comment against the social work values as set down in the National Occupational Standards, and determine how it measures up against them. Steve's surprise indicates that he assumed that Iain would think there was nothing amiss about this behaviour, and anyway this was not Iain's issue. In fact the challenge made by Iain had a profound impact on Steve and gave him the opportunity to have an *autobiographically critical moment* (Mason, 2002, p20) to reflect on the incident, his assumptions, and how another man, whom he liked, viewed his behaviour.

If a sexist, racist or homophobic comment or joke is made, should it be up to those groups to challenge it, as it is at their expense, or do we not all have a duty to challenge discrimination, and form an alliance with groups of people who on a routine basis are discriminated against? Part of Iain's subsequent discussion with Steve revolved around the lack of congruence between Steve's values and those of their social work course. In that moment, Parsloe and Wray's (2001, p173) view rang true for Steve, that:

> *People only take self-development seriously when they recognize either an immediate tangible benefit or a credible negative consequence of not doing so.*

He did not want to lose Iain's friendship, and he started to reflect on his relationships with some of his peers, and whether he accorded people the respect that they deserved. Steve went and apologised to the student for his comment.

Belief systems

A component of developing self-awareness is to identify our belief systems. Cottrell (2003, p38) identifies the use of metaphors to illustrate how we view life (see Figure 9.1). This reveals what our current belief systems are, and whether we generally have an optimistic and hopeful outlook, or whether we have a tendency towards pessimism.

Our belief systems are developed throughout our childhood and adolescence. If you grew up in an environment where there was tension and anxiety, this might have affected your overall view of life, and for you the metaphor of life as a trial or burden may resonate, whereas if you remember your childhood as mainly happy, your metaphors may be about life as fun and a gift. Our philosophy of life is often revealed in how we present ourselves to other people. Koprowska (2005, p41) suggests an activity that enables us to reflect on the messages that we give to others.

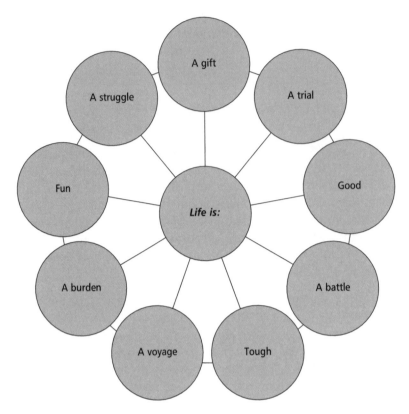

Figure 9.1 Life metaphors

ACTIVITY 9.2

Think about yourself for a moment: what is your usual posture? What is your speed or pace when you are walking? Here are some possibilities (picture the posture and facial expression that goes with each as you read them).

- *Always in a hurry.*
- *Easygoing, relaxed.*
- *Tense, worried.*
- *Cheerful, friendly.*
- *High energy, enthusiastic and excited.*

If you were to ask a friend, family member or colleague, how would they describe your usual posture and facial expression?
What do they think is your life metaphor? Do you agree?

Comment

We all need to think about the impact we have on others. A social worker who looks permanently harassed or irritated will experience difficulty in establishing rapport with people (Chapters 1 and 2). Once we develop self-awareness we can change, and enhance our strengths, and one approach is to develop positive thinking habits.

Managing our thoughts

Butler and Hope (2007, p9) explain that cognitive theory suggests it is our thoughts that determine our feelings, and once we learn how to manage our thoughts we can provoke a positive emotional change. For example, if you have a sudden feeling of sadness you need to ask yourself what were you thinking, what image was going through your mind; in the same way, if you suddenly find yourself feeling elated, what were you thinking about? The way we manage our thoughts is to challenge our internal dialogue, that is self-talk (Back and Back, 1999, p12). This can be illustrated as follows:

Noticing our thoughts

Situation	Feelings	What went through my mind at the time: *what was I telling myself, what images was I seeing?*
Cindy and Don Peters contacted the Team Manager in my placement and said that they were not prepared to see me as I was too young and inexperienced.	Surprise, upset, confused	• I must have appeared incompetent when I first met them. • I may fail my placement.
Joy phoned me and said that I had really helped her to get some things straight in her own mind by listening, and talking through with her what she can do to manage her two-year-old daughter's temper tantrums.	Happy	• I am able to help people. • I am able to get alongside young parents.

You can become aware of your thoughts by noticing what you say to yourself, especially in moments when you experience intense emotions. A feeling is always preceded by a thought. Catch the thought and you will understand where the feeling came from. To develop self-esteem and emotional resilience you need to adopt self-talk that is balanced, proportionate to the situation and supportive, in contrast to self-talk that is critical and judgmental.

Butler and Hope (pp72,74) have identified *thirteen kinds of crooked thinking*, which are very common and most of us at some time have had these thoughts, so you may recognise some of them either in yourself or in other people.

- Catastrophising – automatically thinking that a disaster will happen, for example, *My partner is late home, maybe there has been a multi-vehicle accident on the motorway.*

- Overgeneralising – if something happens once thinking it will happen again, *She is always unreliable.*

- Exaggeration – making difficulties worse than they really are, *I am devastated my team lost.*

- Dismissing positive statements and events, *It was really just a bit of luck that my dissertation achieved the highest mark in the year group.*

- Mind reading – thinking that you know what other people are thinking, *I know what he was thinking, that I am incompetent.*

- Making predictions about the future, *I can see exactly what will happen, it will be a disaster, mark my words.*

- Using extreme language without any balance, *If she doesn't stay with him, he will die of a broken heart.*

- Taking things personally, *I know why I was allocated this case, I'm hated by management.*

- Taking the blame when it is not your fault, *It's down to me that Phillip got hit by Tina. I spoke to her two weeks ago about her aggression.*

- Mistaking feelings for facts, *I like her so much she's bound to like me.*

- Name calling, *What a fool I am. There is no fool like an old fool.*

- Making a situation into a crisis, *What if the plane is hijacked?*

- Thinking things would be better if they were different, *If only I was wealthy I would be happy.*

Are some of these thoughts familiar to you? Have you heard other people express them?

If we keep repeating negative and often fearful ideas to ourselves, these reinforce a gloomy perspective. The good news is that we can change our thinking patterns and beliefs into positive, life-affirming approaches (Seligman, 2003).

Self-talk can be changed by challenging negative thoughts with questions such as:

- What other ways of looking at this are there?

- Am I being too hard on myself?

- What would a friend say to me at a time like this?

- Is there any evidence for my negative thoughts?

- What are the facts?

- What is the worst that could happen, even if things do not go the way I want them to?

- I have coped with difficulties before and I will cope again.

- In six months' time will this matter to me?

CASE STUDY

Gerry started working in a community project for people with mental health needs. Her role was to develop a number of support groups. A priority area that had been identified was for people with depression. Gerry decided to utilise cognitive therapy as the theory to underpin the work of the group. She delivered some workshops that explained the theory to the service users and asked them to keep thought records to become familiar with their self-talk, and to track when they had sudden mood changes. Over time the group became familiar with their self-talk, and developed the habit of turning negative statements into positive ones. They could also identify and feed back to each other examples of 'crooked thinking'. Set out below is one of the tasks that Gerry set the group.

Ways of seeing

	Pessimistic statement	Optimistic statement
1	It never rains but it pours	The sun is always behind the clouds
2	I'm a worrier, always will be	
3	There is too much change going on	With change comes new opportunities
4	Things are bleak	
5	Don't bother trying to improve things	
6	We've tried that, it didn't work	
7	Luck never comes our way	

ACTIVITY 9.3

Take the negative statements that have not been reworded and think how you could make them positive.
How easy or difficult did you find this?

Comment

Seligman (2003) characterises pessimism as a belief that sees misfortunes as permanent, which he defines as pertaining to time and as all-pervasive, which relates to space (p90). Another concept developed by Peterson, Maier and Seligman (1993) is learned helplessness, where the person believes that whatever they do will have no impact. Seligman maintains that optimism and hope can be learnt through challenging our thoughts. So by returning to the statements above these can be characterised and challenged in the following way:

Ways of seeing

Pessimistic statement	Comment about the pessimistic statement	Change to an optimistic statement
It never rains but it pours	Pervasive statement	*The sun is always behind the clouds*
I'm a worrier, always will be	Learned helplessness, Permanent statement	*On occasions I worry, but most of the time I tend to get on with things*
There is too much change going on	Pervasive statement	*With change come new opportunities*
Things are bleak	Permanent statement	*Things are difficult at the moment but nothing goes on forever*
Don't bother trying to improve things	Learned helplessness	*Where there is a problem there is a solution*
We've tried that, it didn't work	Learned helplessness	*Now it's time to resolve this using our previous experience*
Luck never comes our way	Permanent statement	*Most of the time we are very lucky*

Butler and Hope (2007, pp73, 74) identify 'extremist words' that, said to ourselves or other people, sound blaming, create guilt and increase intrapersonal and interpersonal stress. These words highlight Seligman's identification of pessimistic thoughts seeing difficulties as all-pervasive and permanent.

- *I always get asked to do the boring routine things in the team.*
- *I will never be able to change.*
- *Nobody takes any interest in my achievements.*

Particular words add stress and pressure, as in the following examples.

- Should: *I should offer to help more.* We often say this when we feel some guilt.
- Must: *I must do this right now.*
- Have to: *I have to stay here otherwise my manager says the whole service will fall apart.*
- Ought: *I ought to go around and see him.*

If these words are changed as suggested by Dibley (1986), we can see how they empower us, as we are in control and making choices:

- I can choose *to offer to help more.*

- I might *do this.*

- I could *stay here, but the decision* will *be mine.*

- I may *go round to see him.*

Managing stress through our behaviour

We have considered the importance of developing self-awareness and being clear about our values, and how our thoughts impact on feelings. We now need to make the link with behaviour. A significant issue that social workers need to be mindful of is the stressful nature of their occupation, and their responsibility to take care of their health.

RESEARCH SUMMARY

Based on self-reported work-related illness in 2006/07 it is estimated that 205,000 people in the health and social care sector suffered from an illness that was caused or made worse by their occupation. This is 4.9 million days lost to ill health, an average of 1.9 days per worker, in contrast to other occupations at 1.3 days annually. There are particularly high rates for stress, depression and anxiety, followed by musculoskeletal disorders. (Health and Safety Executive website, 2008)

Social workers often deal with uncertainties and complexities. Self-awareness enables us to develop coping strategies to deal with pressures to ensure that our behaviour is appropriate and positive. One coping strategy for stress is the development of assertive behaviour (Thompson et al., 1994). There can be confusion particularly about what is assertive behaviour as opposed to aggression.

Back and Back (1999, p1) give the following definitions.

Assertive behaviour

- Standing up for your own rights in such a way that you do not violate another person's rights.
- Expressing your needs, wants, opinions, feelings and beliefs in a direct, honest and appropriate way.

Non-assertive behaviour

- Not standing up for your rights or doing so in such a way that others can easily disregard them.
- Expressing your needs, wants, opinions, feelings and beliefs in apologetic, diffident or self-effacing ways.
- Not expressing honestly your needs, wants, opinions, feelings and beliefs.

Aggressive behaviour

- Standing up for your own rights, but doing so in such a way that you violate the rights of other people.
- Ignoring or dismissing the needs, wants, opinions, feelings or beliefs of others.
- Expressing your needs, wants and opinions (which may be honest or dishonest) in inappropriate ways.

People do not fit into these categories neatly, and we can all move between them depending on the situation and who we are with. For example, Sonia was seen at work as being 'strong-minded' and assertive in her approach, and the staff team and tenants of the bail hostel where she was the manager thought her approach was fair and appropriate. Her deputy manager Angus was surprised at how different Sonia was towards her adolescent son, who appeared to 'run rings' around his mother. She tolerated his casual discourtesy to her without dissent. This can be explained by returning to people's belief systems. In Sonia's case she has an understanding of what is required in her professional role to support and prepare the tenants to move on from the hostel, but her beliefs about herself as a mother, and what she must tolerate, impact on her behaviour towards her son, which Angus perceives as passive.

People who exhibit aggressive behaviour believe that their own needs and rights are more important than those of others. Non-assertive people believe that other people's needs and rights matter more than their own. In contrast, assertive people believe that their own and other people's rights and needs should be recognised, and that we are all entitled to contribute and participate.

The consequences of non-assertive behaviour

People who behave in a passive manner may be motivated by a wish to reduce conflict and feelings of guilt. Sometimes there is also some pride in putting other people's needs before their own, which can be experienced as being like a 'martyr'. Back and Back (1999) identify the consequences that this behaviour has on the person, other people and practice. Non-assertive behaviour may lead to a lowering of self-esteem and feelings of powerlessness. Anger, resentment, self-pity and hurt feelings can become internalised. This may lead to feelings of stress which are manifested in physical health problems such as headaches and muscular cramps. Ironically, non-assertive people often want to be liked, but their behaviour creates the reverse.

People who are non-assertive show this through their verbal and non-verbal communication. For example, instead of directly asking for something they may elaborate at great length, apologise for the request and their sentences may trail off at the end. Other examples are: putting their hand over their mouth, crossed arms for protection and slouched posture. The metaphor to fit this behaviour could be 'life is a struggle'.

Initially other people may feel sorry for the person due to the lack of agency and seeing them as a doormat, but this leads to feelings of irritation as the person does not articulate what they want or their views. Non-assertive people may be ignored and avoided by others. The effect on their practice is that conflicts are not dealt with and decisions may not be made.

The consequences of aggressive behaviour

The hallmark of aggressive behaviour is a rigid approach to what the person will or will not do. At times other people will admire this approach as it can appear that the person is standing up for themselves. There is a sense of power and control and the release of repressed emotions. In the longer term this behaviour may produce feelings of guilt, or they might start to become cynical and negative in outlook. Other people may dislike the person, avoid them and undermine them obliquely. The life metaphor that would fit this behaviour is 'life is a battle'. Long-term health consequences can occur such as high blood pressure.

Aggressive behaviour in extreme moments can be shown in fast, fluent speech that may be abrupt. Bodily movements are fast, table-thumping may occur, fingers pointed at people, eyes staring and arms are crossed. The person is not always approachable, or easy to be with. This can have negative and dangerous effects on practice, as people may not be prepared to report significant information to the person due to concerns about how it might be received.

The consequences of assertive behaviour

People who are assertive use concise statements clearly stating what it is that they want. They 'own' their views and start statements with 'I' or 'My' and clearly state their preferences. For example:

* *It is my view . . . but what do you think?*
* *I think we should . . .*
* *I prefer . . .*

Statements are to the point and not hedged as they are with someone who is non-assertive. Other people's views are sought; rational and constructive approaches are used to problem-solve, which is underpinned by a respectful and inclusive attitude. People who are assertive have open body language which is relaxed; they smile appropriately and are characterised by their affability, respectful approach to others and consistency in manner. They are able to articulate their views but in such a way that they do not diminish other people.

Assertiveness in practice has positive benefits for service users and carers, as advocacy is more likely to be successful. Partnership and interdisciplinary working is based on co-operation, trust, honesty and openness, where good working relationships can be developed and sustained. Assertive people are more confident and able to take the initiative. Their energy is effectively utilised as they deal with difficulties in a straightforward and immediate way.

In the development of assertiveness, Townend (1991, pp7, 8) has a list of rights. Our own and other people's behaviour can be assessed against them.

My rights

1. I have the right to express my thoughts and opinions, even though they may be different from those of others.

2. I have the right to express my feelings and take responsibility for them.

3. I have the right to say 'Yes' to people.

4. I have the right to change my mind without making excuses.

5. I have the right to make mistakes and to be responsible for them.

6. I have the right to say 'I don't know'.

7. I have the right to say 'I don't understand'.

8. I have the right to ask for what I want.

9. I have the right to say 'No' without feeling guilty.

10. I have the right to be respected by others, and to respect them.

11. I have the right to be listened to and taken seriously.

12. I have the right to be independent.

13. I have the right to be successful.

14. I have the right to choose not to assert myself.

ACTIVITY 9.4

How would you assess your behaviour against this list of rights?
Does your behaviour change depending on the people you are with and the situation that you are in?
If there are occasions when your behaviour is either non-assertive or aggressive, think of three things that you could do to make it assertive.

How to manage situations that create negative feelings

We will now use a case study to illustrate how Jasneet, a student social worker, managed difficulties in her placement.

Jasneet was a third-year social work student placed in a small group home for people with learning difficulties, whose aim was to assist people to develop social and practical skills so they could move on to live independently. Jasneet was 21 years old, small in stature and very slight. She realised that she had to assert herself to be taken seriously by the staff and the residents.

She had a number of concerns about the placement. All the residents and staff were male, apart from herself and one female resident, Pauline, who told Jasneet that she felt isolated and uncomfortable in this environment, as two of the men were constantly seeking her company and had made it clear that they would like to have a sexual relationship with her.

Jasneet noticed that she and Pauline were left to do most of the cooking and cleaning in the home, although this should have been shared by residents and staff working together. Everyone at the home had been very welcoming towards Jasneet, and she had received positive feedback about her contribution from Hugh, her on-site supervisor, but it felt rather patronising as he emphasised how much everyone enjoyed the Indian meals she prepared.

Comment

Jasneet had recently been looking at transactional analysis (TA). Payne (2005, pp195–6) states that people communicate in terms of their parent–adult–child ego states. The ego is our sense of our self and it *manages relationships with people and things, outside ourselves* (Payne, 2005, p76). Jasneet drew a diagram (Figure 9.2) to describe how she thought about her relationship with Hugh. She was the child and Hugh the parent, as he tended to tell her what to do rather than ask her. She felt disempowered by his approach, although he was consistently friendly and approachable but over protective, which prevented her developing her practice.

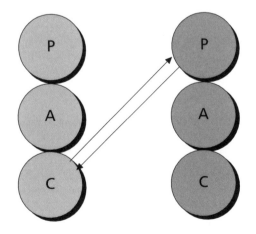

Figure 9.2 Jasneet's relationship to Hugh using transactional analysis

Having established where she saw herself in relation to Hugh, Jasneet explored this further using Harris (1973) and Townend (1991, p7) to set down her underlying beliefs about the situation. Hugh was confident, but did not relate to Jasneet on the basis of equality. She felt there were underlying issues of gender and age difference, and cultural assumptions and stereotypes that Hugh was making about her as an Asian woman. She did not feel OK in this relationship, and thinking about the 'list of rights' she was able to realise that her rights were not being recognised. Jasneet wanted to move her relationship with Hugh so that it was adult to adult. This would enable her to be more influential and safeguard Pauline.

Linking beliefs to behaviour

Life position	Meaning	Type of behaviour
Adult to adult	I'm OK – you're OK	Assertive
Parent to child	I'm OK – you're not OK	Aggressive
Child to parent	I'm not OK – you're OK	Non-assertive
Child to child	I'm not OK – you're not OK	Non-assertive

Jasneet decided to take the following action.

- Discuss the situation with her 'long arm' practice assessor, and request a three-way meeting to discuss her role and responsibilities in the placement.
- Place in writing to the hostel manager, copied to Hugh, her concerns that Pauline was being sexually harassed, and that this was in opposition to the hostel's equal opportunities policy, and adversely affecting her health and well-being (Chapter 8).
- Agree a plan of work so that she could meet the National Occupational Standards.
- Feed back constructively to Hugh about the changes that would need to occur between them, so they could start to relate to each other on the basis of equality and respect.

Jasneet was highly motivated to achieve these changes. Her expectations were that these issues could be resolved, as her approach was focused, positive and optimistic, as she was able to provide the evidence for her concerns and offer suggestions for a way forward.

C H A P T E R   S U M M A R Y

In this chapter there has been an emphasis on the development of self-awareness, and an examination of our beliefs. Links have been made in terms of thoughts, feelings and behaviour, and we have examined the development of assertiveness. Transactional analysis has been considered as one method to assess how we interface with other people. For social workers to be effective they need to be optimistic, creative and energetic. Seligman's (2003) ideas of developing hopefulness for ourselves, and in our work with service users and carers, has been given particular prominence. Making a commitment to our personal and professional development will enhance our self-awareness and our presentation as social workers. Our development is part of our life's journey and of course the journey never ends as we develop as people. What is crucial about any journey is that we enjoy travelling and remember what we have learnt, so our practice is positive, creative and always developing.

FURTHER READING

Back, K and Back, K (1999) *Assertiveness at work* (3rd edition). Berkshire: McGraw-Hill.
This is a highly informative and practical book, which sets out clear approaches to develop assertiveness.

Seligman, MEP (2003) *Authentic happiness.* London: Nicholas Brealey.
This is a very accessible book written by one of the leading proponents of positive psychology. It is essential reading for any social worker.

Chapter 10

Reflective practice
Terry Scragg

Introduction

This chapter will introduce you to the theoretical roots of reflective practice and provide an overview of its main elements and what it means in social work practice with adults. It will explore some of the potential benefits from using this technique and offer you practical ways that you can develop your reflective thinking, record your experience and analyse events, in order to further develop your practice in the context of adult social work services.

What is reflective practice?

The simplest way to understand reflective practice is to start with the word 'reflection'. We see a reflection when we look at ourselves in a mirror. If we use this to make a connection with reflective practice, we are metaphorically looking at our practice in a mirror, in order to consciously learn about our actions during an engagement with a service user, a family member or other professionals, with the mirror reflecting back to us what is going on in a complex situation.

As a social work student your practice will be informed by a range of theories, some arising from your social work course and others from the knowledge and skills involved in different intervention methods such as task-centred or behavioural approaches which you practise during your placements. You will be expected to integrate these theories and skills in your practice when you are in a placement in adult services and later when you are a qualified social worker. But this is only part of your armoury of knowledge and techniques. Both as a student, and later a qualified practitioner, you will begin to construct a body of informal knowledge or experiential wisdom from your practice (Parker and Bradley, 2003). This is where reflection about your practice adds another layer of knowledge and skills to the theories and intervention methods you learnt during your course and while in placements.

In social work alongside other professions, for example education and nursing, reflective practice is seen as an essential skill that all practitioners should develop. Effective social workers are by definition reflective practitioners in that they see reflection as central to their practice and are committed to striving for improvement in their practice. Reflection about and in practice should be developed during social work education and is the key to continuing professional development (Horner, 2004). This questioning approach, which looks critically at your thoughts and experiences, is an essential element in thinking about your practice and deciding how you can make changes in your approach that could improve your practice in the future.

ACTIVITY **1 0 . 1**

Think back to an event that occurred either during your academic work or in practice that challenged your beliefs or values. What was happening in the situation and what was the outcome for you?

Comment

You probably naturally find yourself reflecting on your experiences, particularly if they are new or novel, or you are less confident about your ability to make sense of a particular theory or situation, or where the event stirred long-forgotten memories that may have been painful. This could be termed a common-sense reflection and does not in itself promote learning. Where it leads to learning and development is when the reflective process is structured, ideally through keeping a reflective diary, or through feedback from a tutor or practice assessor, or fellow participants on your social work course. As a result of this process you then act on what you have learned, taking action in the future.

What are the roots of reflective practice?

The notion of reflection as a means of learning through questioning and feedback can be traced back to the works of Socrates, and in the early twentieth century to the work of the influential educational philosopher Dewey (1938) and his view that reflection is linked to solving problems, with a continual re-evaluation of personal beliefs, assumptions and ideas in the light of experience and information, and the generation of alternative interpretations of those experiences and information. The ideas originally developed by Dewey were refined by Schön (1983a, b), who sought to understand what practitioners do through examining their practice, and described two types of reflection: reflection-in-action (thinking on your feet) and reflection-on-action (retrospective thinking).

Reflection during or after practice

Reflection-in-action involves looking at your experience of a situation (say meeting a service user for the first time in your practice placement), connecting with your feelings and thinking about the theories you have learnt about such situations. Where you are faced with a novel situation through reflecting-in-action you are building a new understanding that will inform your action as your relationship with the service user unfolds. In these situations you come to recognise that each service user's situation is unique, but as you build up experience in practice you can draw on what has gone before, while remaining open to situations which you find uncertain or unique. One of the limitations of reflection-in-action is that the timescale can be extremely short and decisions have to be made quickly with scope for reflection extremely limited (Eraut, 1994), and where you have to exercise judgments in fast-changing situations and often under extreme conditions (Ixer, 1999).

In contrast, reflection-on-action is done later, say after your encounter with the service user, typically in discussion with your practice assessor, your peers, or in a tutorial, where you can spend time exploring why you acted the way you did and what was happening during your contact with the service user. In doing this you are developing a set of questions and ideas about your activities and their practice, and through this process you are developing a set of abilities and skills that indicate the taking of a critical stance, an orientation to problem-solving or state of mind (Moon, 1999a, b).

How you can use reflective practice

In explaining how reflective practice can be used, Moon (2004) sees it typically being applied to relatively complicated or ill-structured ideas where there is no obvious solution and which entail further exploration and understanding of a situation. Among a wide range of outcomes that can result from reflective processes she suggests:

- learning, knowledge and understanding;
- some form of action;

- a process of critical review;

- personal and continuing professional development;

- reflection on the process of learning or personal functioning;

- the building of theory from observation in practice situations;

- the resolution of uncertainty or solving problems;

- emotional impact;

- unexpected outcomes, for example, ideas that could be solutions to dilemmas;

- recognition that there is the need for further reflection.

What this process suggests is that you can create meaning and understanding by observing and analysing themes and issues that arise from your interaction with service users and others, rather than applying general principles to individual cases (Schön, 1987).

ACTIVITY *10.2*

Think about a situation that has occurred recently where you met a carer or service user for the first time, and where you felt unsure about how you should respond to the situation as you did not feel you had sufficient knowledge or experience. Using the above list of outcomes from Moon to analyse the situation, what were the main outcomes for you?

Comment

You may have had a range of responses to the situation during the process of reflection, including thoughts about how you felt you responded to the person's needs, emotions about the person's situation and whether you were able to offer sufficient support, or whether your actions seemed convincing to the person in view of their pressing needs. What this process offers is the opportunity to identify those areas of your practice where you feel confident and those areas where you feel less secure and you identify these as areas for further development. An introduction to the process of reflection should help you to realise that you can learn from your past experiences and how new learning can improve and enhance your practice.

CASE STUDY

Debbie, a social worker in a community service for people with learning difficulties, was called to a situation where Tina, a tenant in a supported living scheme, was considered by neighbours to be at risk and where they were pressing the service to find her alternative accommodation. Tina experienced difficulties managing her emotions, although this had improved significantly since she had gained the tenancy of her own flat and a

---

dedicated support worker. Tina attended a sheltered workshop and had been upset as a result of a recent incident, and a neighbour had witnessed an emotional outburst when she met Tina in the entrance to the flats. Debbie felt under pressure from Tina's neighbours to act but resisted this.

Following discussion with Tina and her support worker about the situation, Debbie used the experience to reflect on the situation with her manager, where the tension between 'playing it safe' and acceptable risk-taking were discussed. The value of using reflection for Debbie was the opportunity to stand back and take time to review the situation, using reflective questions to explore an range of possible scenarios that would meet both Tina's continuing need for greater autonomy and control that she was experiencing in the supported living scheme and at the same time reassure her neighbours that the service understood their concerns and was supporting Tina so that she would be able to manage her behaviour.

Opportunities for reflection on your practice

In order to use the techniques of reflection effectively you need the right conditions. These include having space where you can engage with the process of reflection, both on your own, maybe completing a reflective diary, with your practice assessor or university tutor, and in group situations such as tutorials and seminars. Each of these contexts provides different opportunities to engage in the reflective process.

The idea of a reflective space is described by Knott and Spafford (2007) as encompassing space and the time to spend in it. Whether you are a student completing your qualifying or post-qualifying course, you need space to think about your practice, ideally with another person, for example, your practice assessor or university tutor, who can act as a guide to challenge you to examine your practice in a structured way that leads to outcomes that further develop your practice. Similarly, you need reflective space outside of the formal course or employment structure in your domestic life where you need to make your needs known and agreed. Reflective space could also mean using opportunities when travelling or doing other tasks to engage in reflection. Reflection needs to take place, at least in the early stage of your career, in a safe environment where mistakes can be discussed in a blame-free context. It is important that you feel comfortable with your practice assessor or supervisor or university tutor, to speak openly and frankly about your practice, describing what went well and what was difficult. In this way you begin to develop a critical stance in relation to your practice in circumstances where you develop confidence from their feedback. The appropriate conditions for reflection can be constructive and result in self-enhancement, but where conditions are inappropriate then these can be destructive to a social worker's professional and self-development (Yip, 2006).

Your practice assessor or supervisor needs to understand practice, be familiar with the main social work theories and be sensitive to your needs as a learner. They also need to be able to ask the right questions – the who, what, where and when – of practice or events, that will help you to analyse your practice in a way that gives you greater insight and understanding into your actions and those of others. They are not there to come up with expert answers, but to facilitate an increased awareness of the range of possible approaches that you can test out in your practice.

When you start reflecting-on-action, the initial step is to describe the incident that you want to use for the discussion. It helps here if you keep a reflective diary, as you cannot rely on your memory for the details of the events. Recording what took place as soon after the event as possible is important. It is argued by Richardson and Maltby (1995) that the discipline of writing a diary promotes the qualities needed for reflection, including open-mindedness and motivation, self-awareness, description and observation, critical analysis, problem-solving and synthesis and evaluation.

Writing a reflective diary

A particularly valuable tool to help you develop your reflective practice is the use of a diary where you record your experience of practice, for example, using a critical incident analysis to explore an episode of practice in some depth. You could use this to describe the practice episode and your intervention and the outcome. The example you choose could be a snapshot or a more extended analysis in the form of a process recording. This could form the basis of a discussion with your practice assessor or university tutor.

Here are some things you can do to ensure that you commit yourself to writing your reflective diary.

- Set some time aside each week for writing up your diary.

- Give yourself sufficient time to sift through your thoughts and ideas.

- Do not worry about style or presentation (it is your personal diary).

- Report your thoughts, feelings and opinions rather than mere factual events.

- Remember that it should facilitate reflection on your practice.

Reflective questions

You could use the following set of questions to assist your thinking when you are writing up your reflective diary or when you are thinking back over an experience and discussing with your practice assessor or supervisor.

- What was I aiming to do when (for example) I met the carer or person who uses services?

- What exactly did I do? (describe it precisely)

- Why did I choose that particular action?

- What theories or models informed my actions?

- What was I trying to achieve?

- How successful was I?

- Could I have dealt with the situation better?

- How could I do it differently next time?

- Has this changed the way in which I will do things in the future?

(adapted from Allin and Turnock, 2007)

When you are completing your social work degree or post-qualifying course there is a wide range of additional opportunities for reflection where you can explore your practice, including the following.

Supervision with your practice assessor

Your practice assessor will understand the value of reflection as an aid to your development as a practitioner, and structure supervision sessions so that you have ample opportunity to discuss examples of your work with service users, or other events where you have questions about your practice or the actions of other professionals (Edwards, 2007). It is here that your reflective diary can be particularly helpful with its focus on events or situations you have experienced that can be used as the basis for exploration of your practice. This is a particularly important stage in your professional development, as good habits established in placement can be taken forward as you continue to use reflection when qualified.

Other opportunities for reflection on your practice include a critical incident analysis of a particular episode which includes a detailed account of the intervention, and a process recording where a thorough description of an aspect of your practice is used to promote critical analysis (Edwards, 2007).

Consultation

Another area that provides an opportunity for reflection is in consultation (Scragg, 2007). This is a problem-solving process where you use your practice assessor (or another experienced practitioner) as a consultant. The difference between consultation and supervision is that it can be a one-off event, where you set the agenda and your practice assessor facilitates you working through a specific issue that concerns you.

In order to encourage you to test out your ideas, the 'consultant' should not come up with expert answers, but should create the conditions where you become aware of the wider range of interpretations of your practice and the possibilities that you can test out in future.

Seminars and tutorials

These take place in the context of your university course and provide an opportunity to present examples of practice, mindful of confidentiality and other ethical considerations, where feedback from tutors and peers can help you make sense of what is happening in a situation, drawing on the greater knowledge and experience of those taking part. It also an opportunity to test how far learning from practice integrates or challenges theories of social work intervention.

Skills laboratory work

The provision of a skills laboratory, with video facilities and/or two-way mirror, can also be helpful here where the modelling and role play of social work interviewing can provide opportunities for feedback on performance that can enhance your skills in the future (Knott and Spafford, 2007). The skills laboratory can also be used to help replay events where you have concerns about your social work skills and use a reflective example to test out future approaches in a safe setting.

Exploring social work in multi-disciplinary settings

With social workers increasingly working in multi-agency or professional settings, it is important that you have the opportunity to reflect on your practice where you are working with other professions and organisations. This is particularly so where you are working in settings, such as a multi-disciplinary mental health care team, where the dominance of the 'medical model' can challenge social work interpretations and the evidence-based 'social model'. Reflection on your work in these settings, with the support of your practice assessor or university tutor, can help you establish a sense of your own professional self-confidence where you feel you can promote the social model with its insights and understanding of the construction of mental health (Duggan, 2002).

Using a reflective model or framework

I mentioned earlier that it is important that you structure your reflections so that you can evaluate an event in a systematic way that offers the opportunity to analyse what took place – for example, your thoughts and feelings, your actions, the service user's response, etc. One well-tested technique that will help you focus on those elements of practice so that you can structure your reflection is the learning cycle originally developed by Kolb (1984).

Stage 1: Concrete experience

With this stage you should describe what happened to you:

- How did the interaction with the service user progress?

- How did you feel during the interview (your initial reaction, changes in feeling as the interview progressed)?

Stage 2: Reflection

This stage is concerned with reviewing the event or experience in your mind and exploring what you did and how you and others felt about it:

- What went well and what could have gone better?
- What skills and abilities did you use?
- What made it difficult?
- What could you have improved?

Stage 3: Abstract conceptualisation

This stage is concerned with developing an understanding of what happened through interrogating yourself and forming ideas about how you could act differently next time:

- What conclusions can you draw from the experience?
- What have you learnt that you can use in the future?

Stage 4: Active experimentation

With this stage you look at:

- Planned future action.
- What might you do differently?
- What risks might you take?
- Who or what might help?
- What additional support do you need?

RESEARCH SUMMARY

Although research on reflection by social work students in practice placements is limited, an example of research by Lam et al. (2007) suggests that placements provide a rich context for reflective learning, where events that disturb the student, whether these are related to direct work with service users or other professionals. They can act as a challenge and provide the student with an alternative interpretation of their experience, and in turn help them to critically examine their values, ways of acting and assumptions. These events were seen as the main catalyst for students' critical appraisal of practice and the development of improved professional responses. Lam et al. suggest that their findings confirm the early views of Dewey (1938) that problematic issues give rise to reflection.

CASE STUDY

Mr Brown, who has suffered a cerebral haemorrhage (stroke), has been referred to the social work department by the consultant of the unit who considers that he is now ready for discharge following a period of rehabilitation. Yasmeen, a student social worker, has been asked to visit Mr Brown. Following her interview with him, in which she found communication hard due to his speech difficulties, Yasmeen is concerned that he is expressing deep anxiety about leaving the unit and returning home as he is worried he will not be able to cope independently, as he lives alone and has no family support. Yasmeen feels she is being pressured by the nurses and the consultant to make the arrangements for his discharge prematurely. She returns to the social work department to discuss this with her practice assessor.

Comment

This case example provides an opportunity to explore a number of themes through the process of reflection, including Yasmeen's reaction to working with Mr Brown and her difficulties communicating with him and his fears for the future. Other themes are her feelings about being pressured to make a decision that is more concerned with Mr Brown's speedy discharge, rather than his needs, and working in an organisational context where there are pressures on social workers to meet the demands of health-care professionals.

ACTIVITY 10.3

Now you have learned something about the value of reflection practice and how you can use this technique to improve your practice, in this last activity I would like you to think about some of the prerequisite qualities that a social work practitioner needs when they engage in reflective practice. List some of the qualities that you think are essential.

Comment

This is a list is adapted from the Flying Start NHS (www.flyingstart.scot.nhs.uk) web-based material developed to improve the skills of health practitioners that is equally helpful for social workers: You should:

- be willing to learn from what happens in practice;

- be open enough to share elements of your practice with others;

- be motivated to 'replay' aspects of your practice;

- value the knowledge for practice that can emerge from within, as well as outside, practice;

- be aware of the conditions necessary for reflection to occur;

- hold a belief that it is possible to change as a practitioner;

- be able to describe in detail before analysing a practice problem;

- recognise the consequences of reflection;

- be able to articulate what happens in practice;

- believe that there is no end point in learning about practice;

- not be defensive about others' comments on your practice;

- be courageous enough to act on reflection;

- be able to work out schemes to action what you have learned;

- be honest in describing your practice to others.

You will recognise from this list of qualities many of the issues we have explored in understanding reflective practice and its value to the social worker, whether during initial qualifying training or when qualified.

As you become more skilled in reflection and the development of your practice, you will progressively be able to utilise a range of skills when dealing with situations that are characterised by uncertainty, complexity and uniqueness (Schön, 1987), and where you are increasingly able to think on your feet and improvise. This is what Ixer (1999) describes as the conscious control of knowledge so that you are able to self-analyse and learn to operate more effectively in demanding situations, and where you develop transferable skills which are lifelong and not context specific.

Barriers to reflection

We have now explored how you can use the reflective process to examine your practice, and take forward ideas that you can test out in the future, but it is also important to recognise that there can be barriers that inhibit you using the reflective process effectively. Some of these barriers can be in the external environment – people, work settings, or discrimination and oppression experienced. Others can be internal, such as negative experiences, assumptions about your ability, or lack of it, issues of confidence and self-awareness.

Some of the barriers that may affect you include:

- assumptions about what is possible/not possible;

- assumptions about how to learn;

- confidence/self-confidence;

- previous (negative) experiences;

- expectations of others;

- inadequate preparation;

- lack of space or time;

- tiredness;

- ambivalence about a task – do I really have to do this?

(adapted from: **www.ssdd.bcu.ac.uk**)

The value of recognising barriers that may affect your ability or willingness to reflect on your practice is that acknowledging them means you are conscious of the need to work on them. You may not be able to change some barriers, but reflecting on why these barriers exist and why it is not possible to change them can help you learn more about the limits of practice. Similarly, where you identify internal barriers, take time to reflect on what you can do to change things or ask others to help you change or minimise the barriers.

C H A P T E R   S U M M A R Y

This chapter has provided you with an introduction to reflective practice in adult services, drawing on some of the main thinking that has influenced the development of the technique, and some of the settings where it can be used when undertaking reflection on your practice. It also provides you with some practical approaches to using reflection that should enable you to become a more effective reflective practitioner in your work with adults. It is important that you become familiar with the technique and use it throughout your programme of study as this will lay the foundation for continuing to reflect on your practice as a qualified social worker as part of the contribution to lifelong learning and development.

RTHER
ADING

Knott, C and Scragg, T (eds) (2007) *Reflective practice in social work.* Exeter: Learning Matters. This book provides a detailed introduction to reflective practice, drawing on a wide range of approaches, with case studies and exercises that will help you to develop a thorough understanding of the technique and value in developing your practice.

Chapter 11

Skills for self-management
Barbara Hall

A C H I E V I N G   A   S O C I A L   W O R K   D E G R E E

This chapter will help you to achieve the following National Occupational Standards:

Key Role 5: Manage and be accountable, with supervision and support, for your own social work practice within your organisation.

- Manage and be accountable for your own work.
- Manage and prioritise your workload within organisational policies and priorities.
- Use professional and managerial supervision and support to improve your practice.

Key Role 6: Demonstrate professional competence in social work practice.

- Critically reflect upon your own practice and performance using supervision and support systems.
- Use supervision and support to take action to meet continuing professional development needs

This chapter will also help you achieve the following key social work benchmarks (Quality Assurance Agency for Higher Education, 2008):

Skills in personal and professional development.

Honours graduates in social work should be able to:

- manage uncertainty, change and stress in work situations;
- understand and manage changing situations and respond in a flexible manner;
- take responsibility for their own further and continuing acquisition and use of knowledge and skills;
- use research critically and effectively to sustain and develop their practice.

Introduction

In this chapter we will be considering some of the skills necessary for self-management in the social work environment. Social work is undergoing significant change and for social workers there are some skills which need to be added to their 'survival toolkit'. At the heart of the chapter is the concept and implications of the psychological contract between the employer and the employee and the role of the GSCC Codes of Practice for Employers and Employees. The chapter also looks at practical approaches to time management, and an exploration of the management of change. Later in this chapter you will be encouraged to explore the use of supervision and to consider the importance of developing a personal development plan. Maintaining personal safety is also explored in this context to emphasise that the well-being of employees is the joint responsibility of the individual social worker and the employer.

The psychological contract

The concept of the psychological contract emerged in the 1960s but became more popular in the 1990s based on the work of Mullins (1996). Guest and Conway (2002) define the psychological contract as: *the perceptions of the two parties, employee and employer, of what their mutual obligations are towards each other.*

Unlike the contract of employment, which is a legal contract, the psychological contract deals much more with perceptions. Some of the perceptions may be made explicit at the point of recruitment; they derive from informal discussions about 'the way we do things around here', from the views of colleagues already in employment and their perceptions concerning whether the employer is a good one or not, and also through the organisation's approach to performance management and appraisal. The important thing is that these perceptions are believed by the employee to be part of the relationship with the employer. The Chartered Institute of Personnel and Development factsheet (CIPD, 2008) concerning psychological contracts states:

> It is the psychological contract that effectively tells employees what they are required to do in order to meet their side of the bargain, and what they can expect from their job . . . Basically the psychological contract offers a metaphor, or representation of what goes on in the workplace . . . it offers a framework for addressing 'soft' issues about managing performance; it focuses on people, rather than technology; and it draws attention to some important shifts in the relationship between people and organisations.

ACTIVITY 11.1

At the point of beginning a new placement, considering the following questions might help you to engage with your new colleagues and build rapport more quickly.
What unspoken rules do I need to be aware of in this team?
Where does the power lie in this team?
What do people expect of students in this team?
How is the tea fund managed in this team?

Comment

The last question may sound rather flippant, but the state of the tea fund and the way in which it is managed can tell you a lot about the way a team shares or does not share activities.

The CIPD (2008) factsheet also suggests the concept of 'process fairness', which is concerned with people wanting to know that their interests will be taken into account when important decisions are taken; they would like to be treated with respect; they are more likely to be satisfied with their job if they are consulted about change. Underpinning such expectations is the need for managers to be fully committed to communicating with their staff on all aspects of the life of the organisation, which may impact the well-being and expectations of the employee.

The General Social Care Council Codes of Practice for Employers of Social Care Workers and for Social Care Workers (2002) essentially spell out part of the psychological contract. *The [then] National Care Standards Commission and the Social Services Inspectorate will take this code into account in their enforcement of care standards.*

The following are some useful examples of the requirements placed on employers by the code.

- Giving staff clear information about their roles and responsibilities, relevant legislation and the organisational policies and procedures they must follow in their work. (1.4)

- Effectively managing and supervising staff to support effective practice and good conduct and supporting staff to address deficiencies in their performance. (2.2)

- Having systems in place to enable social care workers to report inadequate resources or operational difficulties which might impede the delivery of safe care and working with them and relevant authorities to address those issues. (2.3)

- Providing induction, training and development opportunities to help social care workers do their jobs effectively and prepare for new and changing roles and responsibilities. (3.1)

- Responding appropriately to social care workers who seek assistance because they do not feel able or adequately prepared to carry out any aspects of their work. (3.4)

- Making it clear to social care workers, service users and carers that violence, threats or abuse to staff are not acceptable. (4.3)

Social care workers by the same token are required to be accountable for the quality of their work and take responsibility for maintaining and improving their knowledge and skills.

- As a social care worker you must be accountable for the quality of your work and take responsibility for maintaining and improving your knowledge and skills. (6.0)

- Informing your employer or the appropriate authority about any personal difficulties that might affect your ability to do your job competently and safely. (6.3)

- Seeking assistance from your employer or the appropriate authority if you do not feel able or adequately prepared to carry out any aspect of your work, or you are not sure about how to proceed in a work matter. (6.4)

- Undertaking relevant training to maintain and improve your knowledge and skills and contributing to the learning and development of others. (6.8)

From your student experience you will be aware of the importance of the quality of relationships you have with your practice assessor and your tutor/s. It cannot be overstated how important it is for you, once you are working, to develop a trusting and open relationship with your line manager, who will be responsible for your supervision and support for your personal development, and your team colleagues from whom you will both learn and gain support and friendship.

CASE STUDY

Libby qualified a year ago and has started on the consolidation module of the Mental Health Specialist Award. She is finding the demands of the course and a full-time job very difficult to manage. Libby really enjoyed her social work degree and knew all the way through her qualifying training that she wanted to specialise in mental health. Libby is working in a Community Mental Health Team where she is one of two qualified social workers but she has been taken under the wing of some of the other team members who seem very experienced and confident. The team manager supervises Libby once a month and is encouraging and supportive.

Libby has been feeling quite stressed lately: her caseload includes a couple of young men presenting with very challenging and intimidating behaviour, to the extent she has felt quite frightened when visiting them in the community. Both men live in bed-and-break-fast accommodation in a large former hotel at the seaside. She has not mentioned her concerns to anyone at work as she feels it might reinforce people's views about her lack of experience.

Libby has had a real run of bad luck: she backed her car into a bollard when parking two weeks ago, she was OK but her car needs about £600 spent on it to restore the back end. She lost her purse with all her bank cards a few days ago, and yesterday, to cap it all, she ended up weeping with the mother of a service user who had made a serious suicide attempt.

Libby feels she is not coping very well in her first job, but that it is very difficult to talk to any one about how she is feeling given the job she does.

ACTIVITY 11.2

Write down some of your initial thoughts about what is happening to Libby and why. How might Libby use the psychological contract and the GSCC Codes of Practice to support her?

Comment

There are occasions when even very experienced workers feel intimidated and afraid. Such feelings, however experienced or inexperienced a worker you are, should never be kept to yourself. It is incumbent on you, your line manager and your organisation to ensure your safety. The situation Libby is in with the two service users must not be minimised.

The other side of this coin is about becoming over-confident and not spotting the signals that potentially could put you at risk.

> ### RESEARCH SUMMARY
>
> **Highlights from the National Task Force**
> *The research overview of the work of the National Task Force on Violence (DoH, 2007c) highlights that violence and abuse in social care are significantly under-reported. They comment that the factors influencing the low levels of reporting are believing management will not support staff; that oneself is to blame; that you will be seen as incompetent because you cannot handle violence and abuse; and the belief that verbal abuse and threats are part of the job.*
>
> The consistent message from staff, service users and the research is that violence and abuse should not be seen as part of the job.
>
> *Where social workers have any concerns about their safety, this must be shared with the line manager and colleagues immediately and the operational procedures in place must be followed.*

Work-related stress

In Chapter 9 we considered how our thoughts, values and belief systems impact on our behaviour. This chapter takes a look at the symptoms of stress and the impact the organisation can have on relieving work place stress.

Work related stress is defined as:

> *a pattern of emotional, cognitive, behavioural and physiological reactions to adverse and harmful aspects of work content, work organisation and the working environment. It is a state characterised by high levels of agitation and distress and often feelings of not coping.*

> (Diamantopoulou, 2002 p3)

Diamantopoulou goes on to note that: *It is clear that work related stress is one of the most important threats to workers' well being.*

Cox and Rial-Gonzalez (2002) consider that:

> *People experience stress when they feel an imbalance between the demands placed on them and the personal and environmental resources that they have to cope with these demands. This relationship between demands and resources can be strongly moderated by factors such as social support – both at work and outside work – and control over work.*

Figure 11.1 (Cox and Rial-Gonzalez, 2002 p5) show the known stress-related work factors grouped into ten categories. These different categories, suggest the authors, relate to either work content or work context.

Category	Hazards
	Work context
Organisational culture and function	Poor communication, low levels of support for problem-solving and personal development, lack of definition of organisational objectives
Role in organisation	Role ambiguity and role conflict, responsibility for people
Career development	Career stagnation and uncertainty, under- or over-promotion, poor pay, job insecurity, low social value to work
Decision 'latitude' control	Low participation in decision-making, lack of control over work (control, particularly in the form of participation, is also a context and wider organisational issue)
Interpersonal relationships at work	Social or physical isolation, poor relationships with superiors, interpersonal conflict, lack of social support
Home–work interface	Conflicting demands of work and home, low support at home, dual career problems
	Work content
Work environment and work equipment	Problems regarding the reliability, availability, suitability and maintenance or repair of both equipment and facilities
Task design	Lack of variety or short work cycles, fragmented or meaningless work, under-use of skills, high level of uncertainty
Workload/work pace	Work overload or underload, lack of control over pacing, high levels of time pressure
Work schedule	Shift working, inflexible work schedules, unpredictable hours, long or unsocial hours.

Figure 11.1 Factors associated with work-related stress (adapted from Cox, et al., 2000, cited in Cox and Rial-Gonzales, 2002)

CASE STUDY

On reflection Paul can now see how he had ignored his symptoms of stress for a long time. It was precisely because he had been feeling so low for a long time that it had become the normal way for him to feel. He had begun to feel trapped by his job, and knew that he had changed from being an empathic person to being very detached and rather cynical. His partner had complained frequently about his irritability and apathy and about how insular he had become. It was not until Paul started to have physical

> ### CASE STUDY *continued*
>
> *symptoms that he eventually went to see his GP. He had been having palpitations, which the doctor described as symptoms of anxiety. He also told Paul he was suffering from high blood pressure and that his lifestyle would need to change. The doctor insisted that Paul take sick leave and he was away from work for five months. Paul recently shared his experience with colleagues in a team meeting. He has been back at work now for three months. He highlighted three key things that had triggered his feelings of stress.*
>
> * *Feeling he had to live up to impossible goals he had set himself, which rendered him very susceptible to being asked to take on extra cases at allocation meetings.*
> * *Being expected to be too many things to too many people.*
> * *Having to undertake work that frequently was at odds with his value base and the very reasons he had come in to social work*

> ### ACTIVITY *11.3*
>
> *As part of the team meeting, Paul asked his colleagues to consider the following questions. Answer the questions for yourself.*
>
> * *Do you know when to say no, and how to say no without feeling you are letting people down?*
> * *How frequently do you take a proper lunch break?*
> * *How frequently do you actually leave the building to have your lunch?*
> * *What mechanisms do you employ at work to enable you to switch off from work for a while?*
> * *How often do you have a laugh with colleagues at work?*
> * *Where does your support come from; who is in your support network?*
> * *Do you have a hobby or pastime that you enjoy and can get absorbed in?*
> * *Do you exercise daily; do you eat healthily?*
>
> *Paul feels he could have avoided the build-up of stress if he had considered some of the above issues, but he also feels his line manager could have been more proactive and perhaps thought about providing him with more support at work, a transfer, a secondment, or simply not asking him to take on more cases. Paul was also not aware that the organisation had a confidential counselling service. He would have contacted the service if he had known about it.*

Comment

The one thing that Paul has learnt is he has to assume responsibility for his own health and not wait for other people to rescue him. Paul realises his health and well-being have been seriously affected, but he is also aware that the organisation continued to function during the time he was on sick leave.

The concept of 'Me & Co' at work (Sercombe, 1999, p48) is useful in conceptualising a healthy view of the working transaction:

> *Your boss may be your boss but he is also a customer of yours! When you give good service, keep up to date and work well, if he is a good customer he will pay well in expressed appreciation, good pay, and more opportunities for you when they are available to him. If you do not provide what he wants, or he does not provide what you want in return for your resources, you will eventually find another job.*

Time management

Managing time is an interesting and debated concept (can you really 'manage' time?) but we do know that time passes quickly and sometimes we do not use the time available to us to best effect. The use of time only becomes problematic when we are not delivering on deadlines, when we are letting people down by not keeping appointments or we are causing ourselves unnecessary anxiety because we are pro-crastinating, or we are unable to find the time to be with loved ones.

Williams (2008) identifies three approaches to effective time management.

- Developing ways of working in the same way but working more quickly (scan reading for example).

- Developing ways of doing the same job differently (e.g. having a relevant agenda instead of having an unstructured and unprepared meeting).

- Reconsidering how we think about time, our approach to it and what we value.

Williams (2008 p2) argues that most time-management training focuses on the first two points, tending to emphasise tools and techniques, software and electronic reminders. However, she states:

> *I believe that what underpins effective management of time is a suitable attitude, approach or belief system in relation to time. This influences what is regarded as important, and inspires creative ways of dealing with 'time stealers'...It helps you to make decisions about what to do, or what not to do, and the way in which you might do it.*

Some of you will have seen the 'YouTube' video of the late Professor Randy Pausch's last lecture on time management (Pausch, 2007). At the time of the lecture Professor Pausch was terminally ill, hence the urgency of his messages. He provided some hard-hitting messages about our use of time and some memorable quotes. He talked about the *time famine* and bad time management leading to stress. He suggested doing the *ugliest* thing on your 'to do' list first. He suggested that each of us has creative and less creative parts of the day and that we need to schedule our days to use the creative times effectively. All of us will be aware of the exhortation to touch each piece of paper only once (an impossibly difficult rule to follow) but I was taken with his suggestion not to use our email inbox as our 'to do' list, and to turn off the ping on the email system which signals when a new mail has arrived. As noted above in the section on stress, Professor Pausch emphasises the importance of learning to say no.

Pausch cites Covey's four-quadrant approach to work that needs to be done and suggests the prioritisation of work accordingly (Covey, 1989).

	Due soon	Not due soon
Important	1	2
Not important	3	4

Covey (1989) suggests deadlines *are important, establish them yourself.*

Williams (2008) suggests that changing one's approach to the use of time is fundamentally about wanting to change and being committed to doing so. She suggests the use of the following questions to ascertain one's motivation for change.

ACTIVITY **11.4**

Are you happy with your current use of time?
Are others less happy with your use of time?
If the answer is yes, do you feel concerned about this?
Are you really interested in changing how you manage and use your time? Why?
Do you believe that the change is worth the effort?

Williams also suggests individuals or groups could focus on 'time stealers'. She breaks down 'time stealers' into the categories:

- time stealers that you generate yourself;

- time stealers others inflict on you which you allow to continue;

- time stealers that affect you which are caused by others and over which you believe you have little or no control.

Comment

There is a range of approaches to the management of time, but fundamentally we need to be motivated to change the way we prioritise and undertake our activities. That means reflecting on how we use our time well, and how and why we sometimes succumb to the time stealers. A good starting point is a daily 'to do' list. Make a list of all the things you intend accomplishing each day. Tick them off when you have done them. Start with those things which will not be too time-consuming; a few ticks on your to do list feels quite motivating to do more. Also make a note of the things you have done each day that were not on your original list and ask yourself how and why they crept in. Big pieces of work can be very daunting, so make them more manageable by chunking them up. If for example you are writing a report for a panel, do it in stages rather than trying to do the whole report in one go. Sometimes taking a step back from a report you have started and are struggling with is really helpful in being able to see the wood for the trees. Also remember that things always take more time than you anticipate, so add at least a further 20 per cent to your first estimate.

Coping with change: Getting a grip

In this part of the chapter we are going to focus on coping with change. At times of organisational change, as well as coping with the change programme impacting on the wider organisation, individuals are also required to deliver the day-to-day work of the organisation.

> *Doing something and changing how you do it at the same time is no mean feat and should not be underestimated.*

> *This requirement can be incredibly demanding on individuals and, if not recognised, can lead to severe morale and motivation problems.*

> (CIPD Toolkit, 2006, p11)

The toolkit presents the following explanation of the change cycle which individuals will typically experience: *the timing and depth of the experiences varies between individuals but tends to follow the same pattern.*

- *Immobilisation This is the initial feeling of being 'stunned' and may last for just a moment or continue for some time.*

- *Denial People who disagree with any aspect of the change will spend longer in denial than those who see change as positive. Typically those in denial will behave as if nothing has changed or is going to change.*

- *Anger Although anger can be expressed in a number of ways, in the context of the change cycle, it signifies that people have acknowledged the change.*

- *Bargaining Impacts of the change have been recognised and people begin to consider alternatives.*

- *Depression Nostalgia for the old ways of doing things and old relationships takes hold. Where radical change has taken place, this phase may take a long time to pass.*

- *Testing People buy into the change and start challenging and testing the change under different scenarios.*

Individuals will take differing lengths of time to progress through the different stages of the cycle. It will be much harder, and take much longer, for people who resist or disagree with the value base underpinning the organisational change to progress through this cycle, and many will take the options on offer for leaving the organisation. This creates difficulties for the organisation as layers of experience and expertise are lost.

It is important for social work students to be aware that most if not all statutory social work agencies will either be starting, in the middle of, or concluding major change programmes and reorganisations of service.

CASE STUDY

Charlie is the team manager of a safeguarding adults team which, as well as being subsumed into a new Health and Social Care Directorate, is also being relocated to a new building in the town. The impact of this is that the team will be no longer sharing the building with their children and families' services colleagues or be part of the same department. The team is very apprehensive about the changes.

ACTIVITY 11.5

- *Put yourself in the shoes of one of Charlie's team: what would you want to ask Charlie about what is happening?*
- *If you were Charlie, the team manager, what would you be doing to support your team?*
- *Thinking back to the earlier discussion concerning the psychological contract, how might change of this magnitude affect the employer–employee relationship?*
- *What have been the major changes you have experienced and how did you cope?*

Sercombe (1999, p53) rather descriptively suggests that:

> *We have been thrown into a fast flowing river, and the current is increasing. To hold onto the riverbank will easily tear us apart. How can we survive the trip? By understanding the river of change, learning how to use its opportunities, and adjusting. Trying to argue with the river does not work.*

Taking control: Using your supervision to best effect

The final part of this chapter considers issues around the use of supervision. It considers the ways in which taking control of your learning and development can help you cope with constant change, and help you to find a way forward for yourself, by getting the most from the organisation.

Regardless of the enormous changes experienced within social work, supervision remains one of the key constants associated with good social work practice. Morrison (1993) provides a succinct and enduring definition of supervision.

Supervision is a process in which one worker is given responsibility to work with another worker in order to meet organisational, professional and personal objectives. These are competence, performance which is accountable, continuing professional development and personal support.

Morrison (1996) goes on to define the purpose of supervision, which is to:

- ensure the worker is clear about roles and responsibilities;
- ensure the worker meets the agency's objectives;
- ensure quality of service to users and carers;
- support a suitable climate for practice;
- support professional development;
- reduce stress;
- ensure the worker has the resources to do the job.

Care and feeding of bosses

The following are some suggestions about how you can get the best out of your supervision with your line manager. Professor Pausch calls this approach *care and feeding of bosses.*

- Make notes before supervision covering the areas of work you need to discuss with your supervisor and the outcomes you are seeking to achieve. Share this agenda with your supervisor prior to your supervision where possible.

- Ask if you can make your own supervision notes (your supervisor will almost certainly take notes, particularly noting key activities agreed between you).

- Ask your supervisor if it is possible to meet somewhere rather than their office. If it has to be their office, ask your supervisor if they would mind switching off their phone.

- Make sure you give the impression to your supervisor how much you value your time with them; this will help to make the supervisor think again about how to manage interruptions to your supervision time.

- Never allow your supervisor to feel it is OK to cancel your supervision. This is not about making your supervisor feel bad, it is about you conveying that you, and your supervision time, are precious.

- Ensure that discussion about your personal and professional development does not drop off the supervision agenda because of all the other things that need to be discussed. Alternatively, book a special supervision with your supervisor just to consider your development.

Employers must enable their employees to meet the standards in the code of practice. They must provide training and development opportunities to enable staff to strengthen and develop their skills and knowledge. Thus both social (care) workers and their managers are held accountable for the currency of their applied knowledge and skills and for whether the learning culture provides opportunities for individual and collective growth into job roles.

(Preston-Shoot, 2007, p20)

CASE STUDY

When Rakesh was on placement during his social work degree, his practice teacher was undertaking a Masters degree and the Higher Specialist Award in Social Work. As part of the practice teacher's course she had been asked to develop a personal and professional development plan, which was to form the basis of her learning and help to identify the gaps in her learning. The practice teacher asked Rakesh to undertake the same exercise as she felt it would help him to shape his learning programme for the future, and also help him to articulate a career plan for his future. The practice teacher explained to Rakesh that developing her own personal and professional development plan had helped her feel in control of her learning and had assisted her to see her progression as a worker over the years, and also understand better the periods of her life when she had felt stressed and out of control. Rakesh got a lot from developing his personal development plan and now uses it as a work in progress in his supervision. He is using it to shape his future.

ACTIVITY 11.6

This activity is based on the assumption that people undertaking the development of a personal and professional development plan will build a picture of their qualities, capabilities, strengths and weaknesses both as a person and in relation to work tasks, roles and challenges. The individual's increased self-awareness will help assist personal development and career planning. Additionally, the approach will assist in articulating and overcoming emotional and professional blockages, and assist in career development and hopefully progression. It will also help to meet the GSCC requirements for Post Registration Training and Learning. Self-awareness is essential for us as social workers, and most of us find reflecting on ourselves a fascinating activity.

Seven questions are posed to underpin the personal and professional development planning process. You are invited to undertake the activity as Rakesh did, and start to build your portfolio.

- *Who am I?*
- *What have I done?*
- *What are my current challenges?*
- *How do I learn?*

ACTIVITY 11.6 *continued*

- *How do others see me?*
- *Where am I going?*
- *How will I know when I get there?*

A nurses' leadership paper (RCN, 1996) provides some helpful pointers on areas of personal development which can promote your career development. It emphasises a range of characteristics over and above the expected empathy and technical aspects of nursing as indicating a person with leadership potential. I think they are equally applicable to social work. Personal characteristics included:

- the desire to influence (sometimes they may be angry);
- acting with bravery and taking risks;
- self-motivation;
- recognition of personal limitations;
- acting with confidence.

Interpersonal skills included:

- the ability to facilitate and enthuse others;
- working in a supportive style;
- using authority with discretion;
- the ability to say 'no';
- allowing others to take the praise.

These are good measures that can be used for spotting and developing potential in oneself and in others.

C H A P T E R   S U M M A R Y

This chapter has taken a practical approach to issues of self-management and has developed the theme that the employer and the individual have a shared responsibility for well-being and safety at work. You have been taken through activities which may help you to maintain your well-being and enable you to feel in control of the present and your future. As in Chapter 9, self-development and learning are central as mechanisms for maintaining well-being and equilibrium at work.

FURTHER READING

Johnson, S (1999) *Who moved my cheese?* London: Vermilion Press.
This is a simple story that takes about an hour to read, and uses cheese as a metaphor for dealing with change.

Cottrell, S (2003) *Skills for success: The personal development planning guide.* Basingstoke: Palgrave Macmillan.
An excellent introduction to personal development planning.

Conclusion

This book has explored the skills necessary for competent social work and best practice with adults. The content highlighted concepts and values that inform the application of skills and illuminated complex practice dilemmas. The book aimed to help you think for yourselves about ideas and values that you can use to influence and shape your practice. Central themes have aimed to promote the rights and welfare of carers, people who use services and the benefits of partnership working between practitioners.

Sickness rates *(The Times*, 2008) and the *acute shortage of experienced social workers* (*The Times*, 2008, p4) point to wider organisational dilemmas. Cree and Myers observed that: *Good social work must have an organisational context that allows it to thrive* (Cree and Myers, 2008, p158). In light of this the book recognised that social workers do not act alone and are shaped as much by their employing organisations as by their training and values. The book explored ways to achieve reliable and effective social work interventions within organisations affected by the pressures and challenges of restructuring and perennial budgetary restraints. Yet it is in such environments that good practice becomes even more essential, to safeguard the needs and rights of carers, people who use services and ultimately your own integrity.

In the first part of the book (Chapters 1, 2 and 3) we focused on the foundation skills for social work practice. Chapter 1 reasserted the need for creating meaningful relationships with carers and service users. Chapter 2 focused on how communication can contribute or undermine those relationships, drawing on examples from more complex practice situations. In Chapter 3 the nature of our interventions and attempts at advocacy and promoting participation were challenged, emphasising the need for genuine person-centred planning to promote empowerment. Engaging and communicating with people are at the heart of social work but are given direction by our commitment to empowering practice. The importance of empowerment continued as a primary theme throughout the book.

The second part of the book (Chapters 4, 5, 6 and 7) explored key tasks that you will have to undertake in your interventions with carers and people who use services. Effective assessments are the basis for achieving successful interventions but, as Chapter 4 makes clear, it is essential to identify the criteria for your assessment; are you concerned with gate-keeping or needs or rights or risks? Chapter 5 explored further the factors that impact upon our decision-making process and offered strategies to help guide you through this potential minefield. It emphasised the importance of being sensitive, but critical of external influences and our own thought processes and values. Decisions are increasingly made by multi-disciplinary teams and Chapter 6 considered how to collaborate more effectively with other professionals, highlighting the need for clarity and understanding of the roles of others. It demonstrated how collaboration can enable professionals to become more than the sum of their parts. However, competing perspectives and agendas require good negotiation skills, which are the focus of Chapter 7. This requires sensitivity to power imbalances and an understanding of the others' perspectives to achieve 'win–win' situations rather than impasse or potentially oppressive practice.

In the final part of the book we concentrated upon your development. Chapter 8 explored the potential positive and negative impacts of writing, arguing for an anti-oppressive approach. In Chapter 9 we explored how your values, attitudes and behaviour impact upon how you present yourself. This chapter highlighted the need for self-awareness and assertiveness, factors that will not only enrich your professional development but also your personal growth. Self-awareness requires reflection to produce positive, constructive change. Chapter 10 provided a practical approach to applying dominant theories on reflective practice. Chapter 11 recognised that you require support in developing these complex skills and sought to provide suggestions on how you can utilise support from your peers, supervisors and employing organisations. It will help you to stay a safe practitioner on your journey to becoming an accomplished one.

We hope this book has stimulated you to practise the skills discussed and explore the dilemmas raised with your supervisors and colleagues. The book has focused on the knowledge base of adult services but we encourage you to access the wealth of relevant knowledge within other areas of social work.

Whether you are qualified or qualifying, we encourage you to cultivate and retain a commitment to the knowledge and principles contained in this book and to be prepared to constantly hone, update and critically review the practice of yourself, your organisation and others you work with. Reflection and feedback are essential aspects of such practice.

References

Allin, L and Turnock, C (2007) *Assessing student performance in work-based learning. Making practice-based learning work.* **www.practicebasedlearning.org**

Back, K and Back, K (1999) *Assertiveness at work.* 3rd edition. Berkshire: McGraw-Hill.

Banks, S (2006) *Ethics and values in social work.* 3rd edition. Basingstoke: Palgrave Macmillan.

Barker, R (2003) *The social work dictionary.* 5th edition. Washington, DC: NASW Press.

Bateman, N (2000) *Advocacy skills for health and social care professionals.* 2nd edition. London: Jessica Kingsley.

Beckett, C and Maynard, A (2006) *Values and ethics in social work*: An introduction. London: Sage.

Begley, A and Monaghan, C (2004) Dementia diagnosis and disclosure: A dilemma in practice. *Journal of Clinical Nursing,* 13 (3a), 22–9.

Beresford, P (2008) Viewpoint: What future for care? *JRF Viewpoint* (September 2008, Ref: 2290).

Beresford, P and Trevillion, S (1995) *Developing skills for community care: A collaborative approach.* London: Arena.

Beresford, P, Adshead, L and Croft, S (2007) *Palliative care, social work and service users.* London: Jessica Kingsley.

Beresford, P, Branfield, F, Maslen, B, Sartori, A, Jenny, Maggie and Manny (2007) Partnership working: service users and social workers learning and working together. In Lymbery, M and Postle, K (eds) *Social work: A companion to learning.* London: Sage.

Beresford, P, Shamash, O, Forrest, V, Turner, M and Branfield, F (2005) *Developing social care: Service users' vision for adult support* (Report of a consultation on the future of adult social care). Adult Services Report 07. London: Social Care Institute for Excellence in association with Shaping Our Lives.

Boisvert, C and Faust, D (2003) Leading researchers' consensus on psychotherapy research findings: Implications for the teaching and conduct of psychotherapy. *Professional Psychology: Research and Practice,* 34, 508-513.

Borthwick, A, Carr, E, Hammick, M and Miers, M (2008) Evolving theory in interprofessional education: perspectives from sociology. Paper presented to the ESRC Interprofessional education seminar series. June 2008.

Brandon, D (2000) *The tao of survival – Spirituality in social care and counselling.* Birmingham: Venture Press.

Branfield, F, Beresford, P with Andrews, EJ, Chambers, P, Staddon, P, Wise, G and Williams-Findlay, B (2006) *Making user involvement work: Supporting service user networking and knowledge.* York: Joseph Rowntree Foundation.

Braye, S and Preston-Shoot, M (1995) *Empowering practice in social work.* Buckingham: Open University Press.

British Association of Social Workers (2002) *The code of ethics for social work.* Birmingham: BASW.

BBC News. Country Profiles. BBC. Available at: **www.news.bbc.co.uk/2/hi/country-profiles/default/stm**

Brown, K and Rutter, L (2008) *Critical thinking for social work.* 2nd edition. Exeter: Learning Matters.

Butler, G and Hope, T (2007) *Manage your mind.* 2nd edition. Oxford: Oxford University Press.

Cameron, C (2003) Care work and care workers. In *Social care workforce research: Needs and priorities.* London: Social Care Workforce Research Unit, King's College.

Carr, S (2004) *Has service user participation made a difference to social care services? SCIE Position Paper 3.* London: Social Care Institute for Excellence/ Policy Press.

Casement, P (2002) *Learning from our mistakes.* London: Guildford Press.

CIPD (2006) Approaches to change. Key issues and challenges. **www.cipd.co.uk**

CIPD (2008) *Factsheet: The psychosocial contract.* London: CIPD.

Clark, H and Spafford, J (2001) *Piloting choice and control for older people: An evaluation.* York: Joseph Rowntree Foundation.

Clarkson, P (1990) A multiplicity of psychotherapeutic relationships. *British Journal of Psychotherapy,* 7 (2), 148–63.

Clements, L (2008) Individual budgets and irrational exuberance. In *Community care law reports* 11, 413–30 September: Legal Action Group (pre-publication draft).

Clements, L and Thompson, P (2007) *Community care and the law.* 4th edition. London: Legal Action Group.

Commission for Social Care Inspection (2004) *Leaving hospital – The price of delays.* London: CSCI.

Commission for Social Care Inspection (2005) *Leaving hospital – Revisited.* London: CSCI.

Cottrell, S (2003) *Skills for success.* Basingstoke: Palgrave.

Cottrell, S (2008) *The study skills handbook.* Basingstoke: Palgrave Macmillan.

Coulshed, V and Orme, J (2006) *Social work practice.* 4th edition. Basingstoke: Palgrave Macmillan.

Covey, S (1989) *The seven habits of highly effective people.* New York: Simon and Schuster.

Cox, T and Rial-Gonzalez, E (2002) *Work related stress: the European picture.* European Agency for Safety and Health at Work. Magazine 5.

Cree, V and Myers, S (2008) *Social work: Making a difference.* Bristol: Policy Press.

Crisp, BR, Anserson, MR, Orme, J and Lister, PG (2003) *Learning and teaching assessments skills in social work education.* London: SCIE Knowledge Review 1, 1–3.

Dale, P, Davies, M, Morrison, T and Waters, J (1986) *Dangerous families: Assessment and treatment of child abuse.* London: Tavistock.

Davey, B, Iliffe, S, Kharicha, K and Levin, E (2004) Social work, general practice and evidence-based policy in the collaborative care of older people: Current problems and future possibilities. *Health and Social Care in the Community*, 12 (2), Mar 2004, 134–41.

Davey, B, Iliffe, S, Kharicha, K and Levin, E (2005) Tearing down the Berlin wall: Social workers' perspectives on joint working with general practice. *Family Practice,* 22 (4), 399–405.

De Mello, A (1997) *The heart of the enlightened.* London: Harper Collins.

DEMOS (2008) *Making it personal.* London: DEMOS.

Department of Health (1995) *Child protection: Messages from research.* London: HMSO.

Department of Health (1998) *Modernising social services.* London: The Stationery Office. **www.dh.gov.uk/en/Publicationsandstatistics/Publications/PublicationsPolicyAndGuidance/DH_4081593**

Department of Health (1999a) *We don't have to take this – NHS zero tolerance zone resource pack.* London: Department of Health.

Department of Health (1999b) *Campaign for zero tolerance.* London: Department of Health.

Department of Health (1999c) *National service framework for mental health.* London: The Stationery Office.

Department of Health (1999d) *Recording with care inspection of case recording in social services departments.* London: Department of Health.

Department of Health (2001a) *National service framework for older people.* London: The Stationery Office.

Department of Health (2001b) *Nothing about us without us: The service users advisory group report.* London: HMSO.

Department of Health (2005) *Mental Capacity Act.* London: The Stationery Office. **www.opsi.gov.uk/ACTS/acts2005/**

Department of Health (2006) *Our health, our care, our say: A new direction for community services.* London: Department of Health.

Department of Health (2007a) *Putting people first: A shared vision and commitment to the transformation of adult social care.* London: Department of Health.

Department of Health (2007b) *Modernising adult social care – What's working.* London: The Stationery Office. **www.dh.gov.uk/en/Publicationsandstatistics/Publications/PublicationsPolicyAndGuidance/DH_076203**

Department of Health (2007c) *National Task Force on Violence.* London: Department of Health.

Department of Health (2008a) *The case for change: Why England needs a new care and support system.* London: Department of Health.

Department of Health (2008b) *Transforming adult social care.* London: The Stationery Office. **www.dh. gov.uk/en/publicationsandstatistics/lettersandcirculars/localauthoritycirculars/dh_081934**

Department of Health, Department of Education and Employment, Home Office (2000) *Framework for the assessment of children in need and their families.* London: HMSO.

Dewey, J (1938) *Logic: The theory of inquiry.* Troy: Reinhart and Winston.

Diamantopoulou, A (2002) *Europe under stress.* European Agency for Safety and Health at Work. Magazine 5.

Dibley, J (1986) *Let's get motivated.* Australia: Learning Performance (Aust) Pty Ltd.

Dolan, Y (1991) Resolving child abuse: Solution focused therapy and Ericksonian hypnotherapy for adult survivors. In Myers, S (2008) *Solution focused approaches.* Lyme Regis: Russell House.

Dominelli, L (2002) *Anti-oppressive social work theory and practice.* Basingstoke: Palgrave Macmillan.

Duggan, M with Cooper, A and Foster, J (2002) *Modernising the social model in mental health, a discussion paper.* Leeds: TOPSS.

Dustin, D (2007) *The McDonaldization of social work.* Guildford: Ashgate.

Edmund, NW (2008) *A guide to creative decision making and critical thinking.* The hard made easy book series. **www.decisionmaking.org**

Edwards, C (2007) Reflective practice on placement. In Knott, C and Scragg, T *Reflective practice in social work.* Exeter: Learning Matters.

Egan, G (2007) *The skilled helper.* 8th edition. Belmont, CA: Thomson.

Eraut, M (1994) *Developing professional knowledge and competence.* London: Falmer Press.

Evans, T and Harris, J (2004) Street-level bureaucracy, social work and the (exaggerated) death of discretion. *British Journal of Social Work,* 34, 871–95.

Faulkner, A and Layzell, S (2000) *Strategies for living.* Mental Health Foundation.

Ferguson, I and Lavalette, M (2004) Beyond power discourse: Alienation and social work. *British Journal of Social Work,* 34 (3), 297–312.

Ferris-Taylor, R (2003) Communication. In Gates, B (ed.) *Learning disability: Towards integration.* London: Churchill Livingstone, pp255–85.

Fletcher, K (1998) *Negotiation for health and social service professionals.* London: Jessica Kingsley.

Fletcher, K (2006) *Partnerships in social care: A handbook for developing effective services.* London: Jessica Kingsley.

Fook, J (2002) *Social work: Critical theory in practice.* London: Sage.

Fox, N (1999) *Beyond health: Postmodernism and embodiment.* London: Free Association.

French, S, and Swain, J (2001) The relationship between disabled people and health professionals. In Albrecht, G, Seelman, K and Bury, M. (eds) *Handbook of disability studies.* London: Sage, pp734–53.

French, S and Swain, J (eds) (2008) *Disability on equal terms.* London: Sage.

Gabriel, Y (1998) Psychoanalytic contributions to the study of the emotional life of corporations. *Administration and Society,* (30) 3, 291–314.

Gambrill, E (2006) *Social work practice – A critical thinker's guide.* Oxford University Press.

Gates, B (ed.) (2005) *Care planning and delivery in intellectual disability nursing.* Oxford: Blackwell.

General Social Care Council (2002) *Codes of practice for social care workers and employees.* London: GSCC.

General Social Care Council (2002) *National Occupational Standards for Social Work.* Available at: **http//gscc@org.uk.codes**

General Social Care Council (2004) *Codes of practice.* London: GSCC.

Gilbert, P (2005) *Leadership being effective and remaining human.* Dorset: Russell House.

Gilligan, R (2004) Promoting resilience in child and family social work: issues for social work practice, education and policy. In *Social Work Education,* 23 (1), 93–104.

Goble, C (2008) Developing user-focused communication skills. In Mantell, A and Scragg, T (eds) *Safeguarding adults in social work.* Exeter: Learning Matters.

Goffman, E (1961) *Asylums: Essays on the social situation of mental patients and other inmates.* Middlesex: Pelican.

Gordon, F and Marshall, M (2007) Interprofessional learning in practice in South Yorkshire. In Barr, H (ed.) (2007) *Piloting interprofessional education.* London: Higher Education Teaching Academy.

Gorman, H and Postle, K (2003) *Community care: A distorted vision?* Birmingham: Venture Press.

Gray, B and Jackson, R (eds) (1998) *Advocacy and learning disability.* London: Jessica Kingsley.

Greenson, R (1967) *The technique and practice of psychoanalysis.* New York: International University Press.

Griggs, L (2000) Assessment in community care. In Davies, M (ed.) *Blackwell encyclopaedia of social work.* Oxford: Blackwell.

Guest, DE and Conway, N (2002) *Pressure at work and the psychological contract.* London: CIPD.

Hardiker, P. and Barker, M (eds) (1981) *Theories of practice in social work.* London: Academic Press.

Harris, TA (1973) *I'm OK, you're OK (The book of choice).* London: Cape.

Hawkins, P and Shohet, R (2006) *Supervision in the helping professions.* 3rd edition. Maidenhead: Open University Press.

Health and Safety Executive (2008) *Work related research and statistics.* Available at: www.hse.gov.uk/stress/research/htm

Healy, K and Mulholland, J (2007) *Writing skills for social workers.* London: Sage.

Henwood, M and Hudson, B (2007) *Here to stay? Self-directed support: Aspiration and implementation. A review for the DoH.* Towcester: Melanie Henwood Associates.

Horner, N (2004) *What is social work? Context and perspectives.* Exeter: Learning Matters.

Hough, M (2006) *Counselling skills and theory.* 2nd edition. London: Hodder Arnold.

Hudson, B and Sheldon, B (2000). The cognitive behavioural approach. In M. Davies (ed.) *The encyclopaedia of social work.* Oxford: Oxford University Press.

Hugman, R (1991) *Power and the caring professions.* London: Macmillan.

International Association of Schools of Social Work and the International Federation of Social Workers (2001) *Definition of social work.* **www.skillsforcare.org.uk**

Isle of Wight Council Review of Learning Disabilities Services (2005). Available at: **www. csci.org.uk**

Ixer, G (1999) There's no such thing as reflection. *British Journal of Social Work,* 29 (4), 513–27.

Johnsson, E and Svensson, K (2004) Theory in social work – Some reflections on understanding and explaining interventions. *European Journal of Social Work,* 8 (4), 419–33.

Knott, C (2007) Reflective practice revisited. In Knott, C and Scragg, T (eds) *Reflective practice in social work*. Exeter: Learning Matters.

Knott, C and Scragg, T (2007) (eds) *Reflective practice in social work*. Exeter: Learning Matters.

Knott, C and Spafford, J (2007) Getting started. In Knott, C. and Scragg, T (eds) *Reflective practice in social work*. Exeter: Learning Matters.

Kolb, DA (1984) *Experiential learning experience as a source of learning and development*. Upper Saddle River, NJ: Prentice-Hall.

Koprowska, J (2008) *Communication and interpersonal skills in social work*. 2nd edition. Exeter: Learning Matters.

Lam, CM, Wong, H and Leung, TF (2007) An unfinished reflexive journey: Social work students' reflection on their placement experiences. *British Journal of Social Work*, 37 (1), 91–105.

Laming, Lord (2003) *The Victoria Climbié Inquiry*. London: The Stationery Office.

Langan, J and Lindow, V (2004) *Living with risk: Mental health service user involvement in risk assessment and management*. Bristol: Joseph Rowntree Foundation and The Policy Press.

Lawrence, J (2008) Domestic violence happens to old people too. *Professional Social Work*, August, 18–19.

Lefevre, M (2008) Assessment and decision-making in child protection: Relationship-based considerations. In Calder, M (ed.) *The carrot or the stick: Towards effective practice with involuntary clients*. Lyme Regis: Russell House.

Leveridge, M (2002) Mac-social work: The routinisation of professional activity. *Maatskaplike Werk/ Social Work*, 38 (4), 354–62.

Lingard, L, Espin, S, Evans, C and Hawryluck, A (2004) The rules of the game: Interprofessional collaboration on the intensive care unit team. *Critical care*, 8 (6), 403–08. **www.pubmedcentral. nih.gov/articlerender.fcgi?artid=1065058**

Lipsky, M (1980) *Street level bureaucracy: The dilemmas of individuals in public service*. New York: Russell Sage Foundation.

Lishman, J (1994) *Communications in social work*. Basingstoke: Macmillan.

McCray, J (2003) *Towards a conceptual framework for interprofessional practice in the field of learning disability*. PhD thesis. Department of Social Work Studies, University of Southampton.

McCray, J (2007a) Reflective practice for collaborative working. In Knott, C and Scragg, T (eds) *Social work and reflective practice*. Exeter: Learning Matters.

McCray, J (2007b) Nursing practice in an interprofessional context. In Hogston, R and Marjoram, B (eds) *Foundations of nursing practice leading the way*. Basingstoke: Palgrave.

McKay, M, Davis, M and Fanning, P (1995) *Messages: The communication skills book*. 2nd edition. Oakland, CA: New Harbinger.

McLaughlin, K (2007) Regulation and risk in social work: The General Social Care Council and the Social Care Register in context. *British Journal of Social Work*, 37, 1263–77.

Mantell, A (2006) *Huntington's disease: The carer's story*. Unpublished DPhil, University of Sussex.

Mantell, A and Scragg, T (eds) (2008) *Safeguarding adults in social work*. Exeter: Learning Matters.

Manthorpe, J, Moriarty, J, Rapaport, J, Clough, R, Cornes, M, Bright, L, Iliffe, S and OPSRI (2008) There are wonderful social workers, but it's a lottery: Older people's views about social workers. *British Journal of Social Work*, 38, 1132–50.

Mason, J (2002) *Researching your own practice, the discipline of noticing.* London: Routledge.

Mental Health Review Tribunal. Available at: **http://www.MHRT.org.uk/FormsGuidance/formsGuidance.htm**

Moon, J (1999a) *Reflection in learning and professional development, theory and practice.* London: Kogan Page.

Moon, J (1999b) *Learning journals: A handbook for academics, students and professional development.* London: Kogan Page.

Moon, J (2004) *A handbook of reflective and experiential learning: Theory and practice.* London: Routledge-Falmer.

Morgan, S (1997) *Assessing and managing risk.* Brighton: Pavilion.

Morgan, S (2000) *Clinical risk management: A clinical tool and practitioner manual.* London: Sainsbury Centre for Mental Health.

Morrison, T (1993) *Staff supervision in social care.* Brighton: Pavilion.

Mullins, L (1996) *Management and organisational behaviour.* 4th edition. London: Pitman Publishing.

Munro, E (1998) Improving social workers' knowledge base in child protection work. *British Journal of Social Work*, 26, 793–808.

Munro, E (2003) *Effective child protection.* London: Sage.

Newton, J and Browne, L (2008) How fair is fair access to care? *Practice*, 20 (4), 236–49.

O'Brien, J, and Tyne, A (1981) *The principle of normalisation: A foundation for effective services.* London. Campaign for Mentally Handicapped People.

Office of Public Sector Information (1998) Data Protection Act. London: HMSO.

Oliver, M (1996) *Understanding disability: From theory to practice.* Basingstoke: Macmillan.

Oxford English Dictionary (2008) Oxford University Press.

Parker, J and Bradley, G (2007) *Social work practice: Assessment, planning, intervention and review.* 2nd edition. Exeter: Learning Matters.

Parsloe, E and Wray, M (2001) *Coaching and mentoring: Practical ways to improve learning.* London: Kogan Page.

Pausch, R (2007) *Last lecture.* **www.youtube.com/watch?v=ji5_MqicxSo**

Payne, M (2005) *Modern social work theory.* 3rd edition. Basingstoke: Palgrave.

Payne, M (2007) Performing as a 'wise person' in social work practice. *Practice*, 19 (2), 85–96.

Peterson, C, Maier, S and Seligman, MEP (1993) *Learned helplessness.* New York: Oxford University Press.

Postle, K (2002) Between the idea and the reality: Ambiguities and tensions in care managers' work. *British Journal of Social Work*, 32, 335–51.

Preston-Shoot, M (2007) Engaging with continuing professional development: With or without qualifications. In Tovey, W (ed.) *The post qualifying handbook for social workers.* London: Jessica Kingsley.

Pritchard, J (2007) *Working with adult abuse.* London: Jessica Kingsley.

Quality Assurance Agency for Higher Education (2008) *Subject benchmarks for social work.* Mansfield: QAA.

Quinney, A (2006) *Collaborative social work practice.* Exeter: Learning Matters.

Richardson, G and Maltby, H (1995) Reflection-on-practice, enhancing student learning: The writing of a reflective diary. *Journal of Advanced Nursing*, 22, 235–42.

Roger, K (1951) *Client-centred therapy.* Boston, MA: Houghton Mifflin.

Royal Borough of Kensington and Chelsea (2000) *Managing risk: A practitioner's guide.* London: Royal Borough of Kensington and Chelsea.

Royal College of Nursing (1996) *Developing leaders – A guide to good practice.* London: RCN.

Ryan, J with Thomas, F (1987) *The politics of mental handicap.* London: The Free Press.

Schön, D (1983a) *The reflective practitioner: How professionals think in action.* London: Temple-Smith.

Schön, D (1983b) *How professionals think in action.* New York: Basic Books.

Schön, D (1987) *Educating the reflective practitioner.* San Francisco: Jossey-Bass.

Scragg, T (2007) Working with your manager. In Knott, C and Scragg, T (eds) *Reflective practice in social work.* Exeter: Learning Matters.

Sedon, J (2005) Counselling skills in social work practice. 2nd edition. Maidenhead: Open University Press.

Seligman, MEP (2003) *Authentic happiness.* London: Nicholas Brealey.

Sercombe, A (2001) *Fifty ways to a better life.* Milton Keynes: World Publishing.

Sheldon, F (1997) *Psychosocial palliative care.* Cheltenham: Stanley Thornes.

Shell, R (2006) *Bargaining for advantage: Negotiating strategies for reasonable people.* New York: Penguin Books.

Shulman, L (1999) *The skills of helping: Individuals, families, groups and communities.* 4th edition. Itasca, IL: Peacock.

Skills for Care (2002) *National occupational standards for social work.* **www.gscc.org.uk.codes**

Smale, G (1994) *Negotiating care in the community.* London: HMSO/NISW.

Smale, G and Tuson, G (1993) *Empowerment, assessment, care management and the skilled worker.* London: HMSO/NISW.

Smale, G, Tuson, G, Biehal, N and Marsh, P (1993) *Empowerment, assessment, care management and the skilled worker.* London: HMSO.

Smale, G, Tuson, G and Statham, D (2000) *Social work and social problems: Working towards social inclusion and social change.* Basingstoke: Macmillan.

Smethurst, C (2008) Working with risk. In Mantell, A and Scragg, T (eds) *Safeguarding adults in social work.* Exeter: Learning Matters.

Souza, A with Ramcharan, P (1997) Everything you wanted to know about Down's syndrome but never bothered to ask. In Ramcharan, P (ed.) *Empowerment in everyday life*. London: Jessica Kingsley, pp3–14.

Strauss, A and Corbin, J, (1998) *Basics of qualitative research*. Thousand Oaks, CA: Sage.

Sutcliffe, J and Simons, K (1995) *Self advocacy and adults with learning difficulties: Contexts and debates*. Leicester: National Institute for Adult Education.

Tanner, D and Harris, J (2008) *Working with older people*. Routledge: Community Care.

Taylor, BJ and Devine, T (1993) *Assessing needs and planning care in social work*. Aldershot: Ashgate.

Taylor, I, Sharland, E, Sebba, J, Leviche, P, Keep, E and Orr, D (2006) *The learning, teaching and assessment of partnership work in social work education*. Bristol: Policy Press.

Thompson, N (1998) *Promoting equality*. Basingstoke: Palgrave.

Thompson, N (2000) *Understanding social work: Preparing for practice*. Basingstoke: Palgrave.

Thompson, N (2002) *People skills*. 2nd edition. Basingstoke: Palgrave Macmillan.

Thompson, N (2003) *Communication and language*. Basingstoke: Palgrave Macmillan.

Thompson, N (2005) *Understanding social work: Preparing for practice* 2nd edition. Basingstoke: Palgrave.

Thompson, N (2006a) *Anti-discriminatory practice* 4th edition. Basingstoke: Palgrave.

Thompson, N (2006b) *Promoting workplace learning*. Bristol: The Policy Press.

Thompson, N, Murphy, M and Stradling, S (1994) *Dealing with stress*. Basingstoke: Macmillan.

The Times (2008) Social work sick leave. Wednesday 11/6/2008.

Townend, A (1991) *Developing assertiveness*. London: Routledge.

Trevithick, P (2000) *Social work skills*. Berkshire: Open University.

Trevithick, P (2005) *Social work skills: A practice handbook*. 2nd edition. Maidenhead: Open University Press.

Ury, W (1991) *Getting past no: Negotiating with difficult people*. New York: Bantam Books.

Wall, A and Owen, B (2002) *Health policy*. 2nd edition. London: Routledge.

Walker, S and Beckett, C (2003) *Social work assessment and intervention*. Lyme Regis: Russell House.

Weinberg, A, Williamson, J, Challis, D and Hughes, J (2003) What do care managers do – A study of working practice in older people's services. *British Journal of Social Work*, 33, 901–19.

Williams, T (2008) *CIPD member resource*, time management activities. London: CIPD.

Wilson, K, Ruch, G, Lymbery, M, Cooper, M, et al. (2008) *Social work: An introduction to contemporary practice*. Harlow: Pearson Longman.

Wolfensberger, W (1972) *The principle of normalisation in human services*. Toronto: National Institute on Mental Retardation.

Wolfensberger, W (1975) *The nature and origins of our institutional models*. Syracuse: Human Polity Press.

Yip, K (2006) Self-reflection in reflective practice: A note of caution. *British Journal of Social Work*, 35 (5), 777–88.

Index